NUCLEAR REACTIONS

NUCLEAR REACTIONS

Form and Response in 'Public Issue' Television

John Corner, Kay Richardson and
Natalie Fenton

Acamedia Research Monograph

John Libbey
JL
LONDON · PARIS

British Library Cataloguing in Publication Data

Corner, John
  Nuclear reactions: a study in public issue television. -
  (Acamedia research monographs 4, 0956-9057).
  1. Nuclear power. Social aspects
  I. Title II. Richardson, Kay III. Fenton, Natalie IV. Series
306.46

ISBN: 0 86196 251 6
ISSN: 0956-9057

Series Editor: Manuel Alvarado

Published by
John Libbey & Company Ltd
13 Smiths Yard, Summerley Street, London SW18 4HR, England.
Tel: +44 (0) 81 947 2777
John Libbey Eurotext Ltd, 6 rue Blanche, 92120 Montrouge, France.
John Libbey - C.I.C. s.r.l., via L. Spallanzani 11, 00161 Rome, Italy.

Contents

Acknowledgements

We would like to thank the following institutions and people who helped us in the preparation of this study: BBC North West; the CEGB; Trade Films of Gateshead; Yorkshire Television; Glasgow University AIDS research project; John O. Thompson of Liverpool University Department of Communication Studies and Manuel Alvarado, the General Editor of this series. The BBC, the CEGB and Trade Films generously allowed us to reproduce stills from their programmes.

This study would not have been possible without financial resources, and we are grateful to the the ESRC (Grant no. R000231015) for the support which they provided.

Our greatest debt, however, is to all of the individuals and groups who gave up their time to participate in the project. It would be impossible to identify everyone by name but the various groups are named, and their contributions documented, throughout this book.

Introduction

This book is a report on an ESRC research project which sought to explore some of the ways in which television, and then viewers, 'made sense' of the nuclear energy issue during a period when public awareness of the topic had dramatically increased. The accident at Chernobyl in 1986 and its reported consequences were largely the cause of this increase, but heightened perceptions of the problems of nuclear waste disposal (reflected in vigorous local protests by communities in designated 'dump' areas) and continuing arguments from environmentalist groups about radioactive pollution (particularly at Sellafield, in Cumbria) also contributed. Our research was conducted during 1988/89 but we write this introduction in the Spring of 1990, when the debate on the issue has intensified further, following the economic costings surrounding the withdrawal of the industry from privatization plans in late 1989 and the new and dramatic research on childhood leukaemia in the Sellafield area published recently[1]. Both factors have received intensive television scrutiny in the last few weeks and it is ironic that they have re-configured the debate at a time when the argument about the 'greenhouse effect' and the use of fossil fuels seemed to be giving new confidence to the nuclear lobby.

As media researchers interested in television's centrality to modern public knowledge and in the various expositional and aesthetic possibilities drawn on to address and inform the public, we wanted to examine some of the significatory and interpretative work that was being put in to make 'nuclear energy' *mean* televisually.

We knew that the issue was receiving conflicting audio-visual treatments across the range of broadcast, promotional and 'independent' activities, reflecting con-

---

1   *A report by Martin Gardner of Southampton University, linking cases of leukaemia in children with their fathers' exposure to radiation as workers at Sellafield was extensively reported in the press and on TV and radio. See* The Times *17 February 1990: 'Prospective fathers "need shielding"'; 19 February 1990: 'Nuclear power operators face huge leukaemia claims'; 23 February 1990 'Radiation damage "could last generations"'. A good contextualising summary of the report's findings was published in May 1990 – see* The Times Higher Education Supplement *18 May 1990: 'Crushed by lightness of evidence'.*

flicts of opinion in the broader public debate and in the scientific community itself. We were interested, too, in the way in which the debate was characterised by having at its centre a number of highly esoteric technological, scientific and medical questions, making public comprehension, let alone judgement, difficult and thereby giving mediation functions a particular salience.

So the research has a dual 'edge' – cutting equally into questions about TV as a form of public communication, grounded in particular institutional relations and conventions, and ones about the public meanings which had gathered around nuclear energy at the time. The selection of the energy issue is not, therefore, just an 'example' allowing us to extrapolate off into a general theory of public-issue television, nor is it a substantive focal point in relation to which questions of media discourse are secondary. Our view is that it would be no bad thing if such a duality were to be tried more often in the media research field.

Our project involved, first of all, the selection of sample programmes and tapes using different modes of address and exposition and engaging with the topic of nuclear energy from different perspectives. These were investigated comparatively and an attempt made to identify and discuss their overall rhetorical design, their local mechanisms of signification and the key themes which they appeared to project. Sample viewer groups from very different social and professional backgrounds were then used for respondent discussion sessions, involving taping and subsequently transcription.

Analytically, our study connects with two developing areas of media research, that concerned with non-fiction television discourse and that concerned with the study of 'reception' – with the study, that is, of the interpretative activities by which viewers comprehend and attach significance to what they see and hear. Response and, indeed, understood meaning itself may vary considerably as a consequence of audience members drawing upon different schemes of prior knowledge and predisposition. Many published studies have attempted both to plot and to account for such variation and our study includes an attempt to do this in respect of the chosen topic and material. Reception studies, focussed in the first instance not on 'influence' but on 'meaning', have become over the last decade an important element in television research. They have attracted a good deal of investigative effort and an even larger literature of theoretical commentary[2] and we discuss aspects of this in Chapter Four.

The second area of research which we wish to develop is the analysis of TV's expositional discourses. For just as programme analysis without a connection with viewer activity is severely limited in explanatory range, so is a reception

---

2 *A number of recent and useful surveys of the field, including critical commentary on concepts and methods, can be found in Ellen Seiter et al (eds)* Remote Control; Television, Audiences and Cultural Power *London, Routledge 1989.*

study that is not connected back to a detailed engagement with the significatory forms of particular programmes and generic conventions. In our study, we hoped to find out more about those modes of address, devices of visualization and of interaction (for instance, presenter speech-to-camera in a location setting, the uses of unobtrusively 'observational' sequences and of interview segments) which form the grammar of non-fiction television. Through either a misplaced quest for a general theory of television discourse or through the recent emphasis on the analysis of fictional forms, such practices seemed to us to be relatively under-researched.

The reader will find the research presented below in five chapters of varying length. Each of the main analytic chapters begins with a general commentary on our ideas and methods, developing in further detail the points outlined above.

In Chapter 1 we discuss how nuclear energy became a public issue in Britain and look at some of the principal conflicts of scientific and political opinion affecting its development. We also refer to the accidents at Three-mile Island in the United States and at Chernobyl in the Soviet Union which were to be given 'datum' significance by much subsequent commentary.

In Chapter 2 we examine four selected programmes in detail, focussing on their use of language and image to depict nuclear energy and to give access to, and frame, differing perspectives on its safety. We also indicate something of their production backgrounds.

In Chapter 3 we pursue aspects of the programmes further by identifying four principal themes articulated variously within them. We explore both the discursive organisation of these themes and their significance for the nuclear debate.

In Chapter 4 we turn to the viewers, and offer as full an account as space will allow of nine selected groups, with further reference to the full range of respondents studied. We hope that this form of presentation provides clarity in comprehending the relationships between programme elements and particular interpretations and in regarding the comments of respondents as *situated speech*.

In Chapter 5 there is an attempt to cross-connect interpretative schemes and to correlate variations in interpretative framing with the different agendas and social and political characteristics of the groups sampled. Key points of convergence as well as of variation are listed and discussed and there is a note on aspects of respondent speech. Finally, we offer a brief, concluding summary of our project, suggesting its value, its shortcomings and those aspects of its organisation and findings upon which we think future research might usefully build.

1 Nuclear energy in Britain: the formation of an issue

When we began planning this project in 1987 and picked nuclear energy as the public issue that we would concentrate upon, it was as a suitably controversial subject matter. In 1987 it was clear that the nuclear industry did not enjoy the general and complete confidence of the British public. It was also clear that the industry saw this lack of public confidence as a threat to its viability, and was making a considerable effort to counter its bad image with a public information/public relations campaign. This took such forms as a 'Visitor's Centre' at British Nuclear Fuels site at Sellafield in Cumbria, advertised on national television as a tourist attraction; public information packs and videos and touring exhibitions. These efforts on the industry's part are continuing; meanwhile its position has weakened considerably. The following account will incorporate references to developments which have taken place since the fieldwork stage of the research. But we can start by indicating some of the parameters of the public debate at the end of 1987/beginning of 1988, about 18 months to a year after the major disaster at Chernobyl in the Soviet Union.

At this time, there appeared to be four separate issues which constituted 'the nuclear energy debate': the question of health hazard (particularly leukaemia); the risk of a Chernobyl-scale disaster; the problem of waste disposal and the argument about the relative costs of nuclear and fossil fuel electricity. There was a related concern in some quarters about the links between civil and military nuclear operations.

Childhood leukaemia clusters had been found around the Sellafield plant and at other nuclear installations. Considerable controversy surrounded these findings, and medical experts are still looking for a *causal* explanation, despite the recent developments noted in the Introduction. The hypothesis that the illnesses were brought about by ionising radiation discharged at Sellafield is not the only explanation on offer. This issue broadened out into the more general one of health risks from regular radioactive discharges at nuclear establishments.

The 'Chernobyl factor' loomed large in 1987. This accident gave evidence of how widespread the consequences of such a disaster could be. A cloud of radioactive dust and gas was blown across Europe, including Britain, and the Government's actions in advising and protecting the population formed one subject of debate in the months following the accident. This may be incidental to the nuclear debate 'proper' but it did raise the question of contigency plans in the event of a comparable catastrophe in this country. Inevitably, the public became concerned about the risk of such an event. Citizens were reassured that the pressurised water reactor planned for Sizewell in Suffolk (the 4-year inquiry under Sir Frank Layfield was nearing completion at the time of the disaster) was of a reliable American design (by the Westinghouse company), wholly unlike the design used in the Soviet Union.

A third area of controversy at this time related to the continuing search for an inland site where disposal of low-level waste could be carried out. It was in 1987 that the idea of using shallow trenches was abandoned in favour of deep disposal. The Government agency Nirex had been commissioned to explore the possibility of the former at three sites in Britain, one of which would be selected if it proved suitable. But geological suitability was never discovered. Local protest – with health risk as its main concern – was sufficient to make the Government rethink the policy. Further consultation between Nirex and the local authorities followed. The result was to recommend geological explorations at Sellafield and at Dounreay in Scotland (the site of Britain's fast-breeder programme), with the intention of using one or other of these for deep disposal.

A fourth problem for the nuclear industry, albeit rather less prominent in general public debate than the above, concerned the economics of the industry and the challenge to the traditional case that nuclear electricity was or would be cheaper than fossil fuel electricity. At one level, the memory of 1950s hyperbolic claims about electricity 'too cheap to meter' haunted the debate, though the real test was the more modest one of comparability with traditional sources. The arguments are complex. The inclusion of building and decommissioning costs for nuclear plant are thought by the industry to give an *unfairly* inflated figure for nuclear electricity. The industry strengthens the comparison in favour of nuclear fuel by talking about the expense involved in limiting the emission of 'greenhouse gases' from coal-burning stations to make them more environment-friendly. This argument has been developed as the dangers of global warming have become more generally known and accepted for the purposes of policymaking. The industry has to convince the Government as well as the public of nuclear energy's value for money. The Conservative Government was wary enough of the economic case not to rely on that alone, but to stress also a diversity-of-fuel-supply argument as part of its policy of keeping a nuclear capacity in Britain.

Since completing the fieldwork on which this study is based there have been further developments which have pushed the industry into crisis, despite the best efforts of its public information/public relations machine. A moratorium upon the building of new nuclear plant (excepting Sizewell B) has come into effect and will be reviewed in 1994. Sizewell B may be the last nuclear reactor to be built in this country, whilst the process of decommissioning the oldest reactors has already begun. It is primarily the problem of costs, not the risk issues, which have brought about this crisis. The Government decided, at a late stage of the parliamentary proceedings, to exclude all nuclear plant, not just the oldest (Magnox) reactors as had been previously planned, from the provisions for privatising the electricity supply industry. Electricity production could, it seemed, only be made to look attractive to private investors if the expensive nuclear element remained in public hands. Thus, the Government was treating nuclear power as a costly but necessary liability, a stance which could only further weaken the standing of the industry. It was this decision which brought about the resignation of Lord Walter Marshall, chairman of the Central Electricity Generating Board, and chairman-designate of National Power, one of the two private companies formed to take over from the CEGB upon privatisation, and a strong supporter of the nuclear industry.

There have also been significant developments around the health risk issue. Parents of leukaemia sufferers in West Cumbria found a vigorous champion in a local solicitor, and court proceedings were commenced against British Nuclear Fuels Limited. The plaintiffs' hand was strengthened when, in February 1990, a medical report was published showing a strong *statistical* correlation between Sellafield leukaemia cases and the radioactive dose exposure of the fathers of these children, working at the plant.[3] The correlation thus indicated a *possible* causal explanation – that the disease was brought about through the effects of radioactivity upon the genes in the male sperm.

It would be foolish to predict that nuclear energy is finished in Britain. Its advocates may yet win the day – public hostility may weaken, 'green' opinion may become more equivocal in comparing the environmental risks of the various fuel sources, the industry may convince a jury that Sellafield radiation was not the cause of the local leukaemias. But these are not easy tasks and it is just as likely that the next few years will give the anti-nuclear lobby a stronger hand, particularly if the court case produces a victory for the plaintiffs.

---

3 *See Introduction, footnote 1.*

2   The Programmes

Introduction

As we have outlined above, our intention in this study was not only to investigate viewer responses to a specific 'public issue' as depicted through television/video discourse, but also to look at different depictions of this issue and at different methods and devices of depiction. Thus, the research, rather than holding the idea of 'television' constant in order to explore response, would also explore variables both in the rhetorical intentions and discursive operation of sample programmes. In this respect, the precedent set by Schlesinger, Murdock and Elliott in their study of the various generic frameworks within which ideas about 'terrorism' were articulated on television, was a useful one to have.[4] Our study, given its primary commitment to conducting research with sample viewers, was less wide-ranging than theirs in generic analysis. We chose to focus on accounts structured within the conventions of the current-affairs documentary, the form in which most of television's contribution to public understanding of the nuclear-energy issue has been organised. In the first phase of our research, we took the third and final programme in the series *Taming the Dragon*, transmitted in the BBC2 *Brass Tacks* slot in October 1987. This programme, entitled *Uncertain Legacy*, was a critical investigation of the health risks consequent upon the nuclear industry's day to day operations and its problems with waste disposal. It featured accounts both from the industry and its critics.

In some contrast to this, we also took *Energy – The Nuclear Option*, a promotional videotape produced by the Central Electricity Generating Board (CEGB) in 1987 as part of its campaign to win back public opinion after the massive loss of confidence occasioned by the Chernobyl disaster. In much of its design, this video followed the model of broadcast current-affairs output. Using Brian Walden as its presenter/interviewer, it imitated several features of London Weekend Television's highly successful *Weekend World* series. The video, like the BBC programme, also included sustained address to the question of risk. Among other

---

4   *Philip Schlesinger, Graham Murdock and Philip Elliott* Televising 'terrrorism': political violence in popular culture.. *London, Comedia 1983.*

things, it was the potential tension between its use of a model of impartial inquiry and its requirement to convey a promotional message which was of interest to us.

A third item was also taken from video distribution. This was an item from the innovative 'video journal' *Northern Newsreel*, produced regularly by Trade Films of Gateshead and distributed nationally to organisations within the Trade Union and Labour movement. *Northern Newsreel 9*, distributed in 1988, contained a short feature, entitled *From Our Own Correspondent*, about the dangers of nuclear energy. Using a dramatised-documentary method, the piece developed a scenario about a disaster at Hartlepool Nuclear Power Station, making imaginative and direct use of the Chernobyl precedent and coming to strongly negative conclusions about the industry.

These three programmes, connected comparatively and contrastively in terms of institutional origin, disposition towards the topic and discursive means, provided the basis for the first phase of our analysis. In a much briefer, second phase of study, we took an edition of the regular Sunday BBC current-affairs programme *Heart of the Matter* as a focus. During the course of our research in 1989, a programme from this series had looked at the question of the incidence of child leukaemia in the Sellafield area and at the starting of legal proceedings against British Nuclear Fuels Limited (BNFL) by a group of afflicted families. By its concentration upon one specific case-history, its direct address to questions of proof and probability – which were emerging as key factors in our analysis – and its up-dating of the terms of public debate, we found this programme a useful complement to the ones chosen earlier.

In thinking about how these programmes variously related both 'upwards', to the larger current debate about nuclear power in Britain, and 'downwards', to the specific forms of viewer understanding and response, we found the notion of 'textualisation' a helpful idea. This seemed to us to give proper emphasis to the *processes* of selective transformation at work as evidence, ideas, images and speakers from the world anterior to television were processed and assembled within different, self-contained rhetorical systems – the four programmes.[5] We wanted to investigate some of the key variables of textualisation at the level of programme images and speech. However, it was the interaction of such different rhetorical systems with viewers' own knowledge and assessments that was of primary interest to us, and this constituted in a sense a 're-textualisation', as the localised interpretations and responses of various acts of viewing transformed

---

5 *In a recent article we have given three of these programmes a more, detailed comparative analysis in respect of the 'risk' issue. See John Corner, Kay Richardson and Natalie Fenton, 'Textualising Risk: TV discourse and the issue of nuclear energy'.* Media, Culture and Society, *v 12 n 1, 1990 pp 105-124.*

the elements of programme signification back into the realm of public significance.

Thus our research, though it is concerned with the 'textualisation' of only one issue, connects with a number of much more general questions concerning the public communication of policy debate and the processes of informational television. That said, it might be worth noting here how distinctive the nuclear energy debate in Britain might be when compared with other 'public issues' treated by the media. For a start, the documented drop in public confidence in the industry, occasioned by the Chernobyl disaster, produced a situation in which journalistic attitudes towards 'official' positions were possibly more confident in their scepticism and interrogatory vigour than was the case in other areas of public policy. Increasingly, this has become true of the whole area of environmental decision-making. Secondly, the nuclear power debate hinged on questions of scientific judgement which put 'expert knowledge' in a position of centrality to most of the issues at stake, requiring at least as much *trust* as *agreement* from the majority of the population. It follows that viewers were likely to be more than usually dependent on the mediations offered by television – its processings of the debate – for meaningful access to the issue. Finally, television treatments of this topic clearly drew not only on established conventions for engaging with a public issue but on TV conventions for depicting Science – its use of hypotheses, its methods, its often awesome technological hardware and, perhaps above all, its ways of assessing evidence and proof.[6]

The following analytic accounts of the four programmes further develop most of the above points. In them, we have attempted to identify and discuss aspects both of the communicative design and the thematic development of the four items which we used with our viewer groups. We have chosen to separate our accounts into sub-sections in order get greater coherence into our discussion of 'form' and 'content' respectively, though we realise that this is a distinction which carries the risk of ignoring the interpenetration of the two in the actual production and interpretation of discourse. Our accounts are partly descriptive and partly analytical, and since it will not be easy for readers to see the programmes for themselves we have tried at all points to balance these two tasks. In developing these analyses, we used transcripts of programme speech and detailed shot-lists prepared from video copies of the material.

The accounts are organised under three headings: *communicative design, thematic development*, and *visualisation*. Under *communicative design* we discuss key features of each item's rhetorical organisation, with reference to the terms of its

---

6   *See especially, Roger Silverstone 'The right to speak: on a poetic for television documentary'* Media, Culture and Society *v 5 n 2 1983 pp 137-154 ; Roger Silverstone, 'The agonistic narratives of television science' in John Corner (ed)* Documentary and the mass media *London, Edward Arnold 1986 pp 81-106.*

address to the audience. Under *thematic development* we review the programmes from a more substantive perspective, indicating which aspects of the nuclear debate are foregrounded in each case, and how they are treated. In the case of *Uncertain Legacy* and *From Our Own Correspondent* we have also used the heading of *visualisation* to talk about the contribution of visual images to the programmes, since here visual material makes a notably strong contribution to the overall meanings.

Uncertain Legacy – ('Taming the Dragon' Part 3, BBC 2)

The three-part series from which this programme is taken was screened approximately eighteeen months after the disaster at Chernobyl (Part 3, October 22nd 1987). The preceeding parts dealt with the history of the nuclear industry in Britain, particularly its safety record, and with the economic case for nuclear energy, which it challenged. The connection between civil and military nuclear operations is also explored in the second part. All three parts are both written and narrated by the journalist David Taylor who, as a high-profile presenter (appearing on-camera as well as in voiceover), sets out on a *quest* for satisfactory answers to important questions which the public are, or should be, concerned about.

The journalist's quest is at the centre of *Uncertain Legacy*'s communicative design. The formal 'mix' within the programme gives us voiceover film from the environs of various British nuclear locations including Sellafield, Hinkley Point in Somerset and Trawsfynnedd in North Wales; expositional sequences with David Taylor on location; archive footage relating to Hiroshima, Windscale and Three-mile Island; interviews with public figures (Cecil Parkinson, the then Energy Secretary in the Conservative government, Lord Marshall the then Chairman of the CEGB), scientists (John Goffman, a specialist on reprocessing technology, Marion Hill of the National Institute for Radiological Protection) and ordinary people.

The thematic development of *Uncertain Legacy* foregrounds the question of risk. It is a programme which, whilst recognising the ultimate inconclusiveness of the probabilistic, statistical reasoning upon which the risk argument hinges ('You can prove anything with statistics' Taylor says at one point) is nevertheless organised to bring out the coherence, credibility and resonance of fears that arise in contemplating the nuclear industry. It offers an account which operates on the propositional level by engaging with the arguments and evidence regarding discharges of ionizing radiation at nuclear plants and the possible effects of those discharges. There is in addition a strong affective dimension to the text operating through its visualisations, both with and without the reinforcement of commentary.

Fig. 1. *Uncertain Legacy*: Schoolchildren near Hinkley Point learn about nuclear power.

Fig. 2. *Uncertain Legacy*: The surface of the 'warmest lake in Britain', with Trawsfynnedd nuclear power station at its edge.

1. Communicative design

Uncertain Legacy has a strong authorial line, delivered by its presenter. It is not a line which insists emphatically that the risks are real (as Walden in the CEGB tape insists that they are unreal – see below) but one which refuses to accept official reassurances and digs more deeply into the evidence. The programme's closing statement is actually a *question:*

> The case for nuclear power rests upon a balance between benefit and risk. But how can we draw that balance when the risk is so uncertain?

Scepticism is a also a feature in the questioning of official spokespersons and in the framing, prospective or retrospective, of interview sequences. Lord Marshall, for instance, is asked whether he would be prepared to live in the vicinity of a nuclear power plant or waste dump. He says he would – Taylor points out he doesn't. The interview ends with Marshall contrasting the minimal amounts of industry-produced radiation with the enormous amounts of natural background radiation. Radiation can't be bad for you, we are to infer, since 'God put it there' – into 'everyone's house' and 'everyone's garden'. But in cutting from the interview sequence to a shot of a mist-covered lake this argument is sceptically reframed by Taylor:

> If there's radioactivity in this garden, there's a great deal more of it in this lake. And it's not God but the CEGB that put it there.

This introduces a sequence at Trawsfynnedd in North Wales, the only power station in Britain which does not discharge water out to sea. We are invited to witness the 'ghostly beauty' of Trawsfynnedd lake whilst being told that what we are seeing on its surface is not mist, but steam rising from the 'warmest lake in Britain.' It provides water for the plant's cooling system so it is *hot* water which is eventually returned to the lake. What Taylor actually says is that 'Its ghostly beauty is created by the discharge of thousands of gallons of radioactive effluent from Trawsfynnedd nuclear power station'. At the propositional level, therefore, the text is open to question but only from viewers sufficiently well informed to entertain the possible counter-argument that cooling-system water is the only significant 'effluent' and that this never comes into contact with radioactive materials (only one viewing group – of Heysham power station workers – argued from this claim).

2. Thematic development

The propositional discourse of *Uncertain Legacy* deals in explicit and direct terms with the theme of 'risk'. We give this discourse extended commentary in Chapter 3, under the heading of 'proof and probability'. A more implicit construction of threat is also apparent, particularly in the programme's favourite motif of discrepancy between normal appearance and abnormal reality. The danger, ionizing radiation, is invisible and undetectable except with suitable scientific instruments – the geiger counter, the bodyscanner, both of which we are shown in the course of the programme. This motif is introduced in the opening sequence via a classroom scene, during a lesson on energy sources. The viewer is not long left to suppose that this is the normal classroom it appears to be. These are the children of Stogurssey Primary, for whom the government has supplied potassium iodate tablets to be taken in the event of an accident at nearby Hinkley Point. Thyroid glands can be protected in this way from the worst effects of ionizing radiation. There is no doubt that 'threatened innocence' makes for a powerful *emotional* appeal: yet there is also a more 'propositional' reading of the episode which enhances (albeit indirectly) the risk argument. The government itself evidently believes there is something to fear, in the very fact that it makes special provision for the protection of Stogurssey (we are also told that the village's population size has been officially restricted).

3. *Visualisation*

Whilst much of the footage of this production is straightforwardly denotative of the people and places to which the narration refers, the possible affective reson-ances of particular images cannot be overlooked. When the text is playing its strongest propositional card (it indicates that the data on Japanese A-bomb victims now suggests that the standard 'safe' radiation dose limits have been set too low) it gives us archive images of devastated Hiroshima and of victims receiving clinical care. Some respondents specifically objected to this footage as inappropriate in a programme about *civil* nuclear technology.

The visual imagery of the Trawsfynnedd lake sequence (see above) can also be seen as contributing significance over and above its value as photographic evidence – especially when the camera goes underwater and, over the murky screen image, we learn that 'Beneath its surface lies buried a whole spectrum of radionucleids – plutonium, cobalt, caesium, amaryssium – some of which will last virtually for ever, polluting the lower depths'.

Imagery of *deformation/perversion* of the natural order is also an ingredient in the overall mix, specifically in footage from an American-made documentary on the effects of the Three-mile Island disaster. Here we see, and hear about, malforma-tions and sickness of plant, animal and human life. Images of *excess* contribute to the programme's warning that the problem of nuclear waste is still unsolved: 'They can load it all on to a train but they cannot tell the train driver where to go'. One of the pictures in this sequence evokes the daunting scale of the disposal problem by panning across column after column of metal drums which entirely fill the screen. The boundaries of the stack are always out of frame, conveying perhaps the limitlessness of the waste problem itself.

Energy – The Nuclear Option (CEGB Film and Video Library)

The primary aim of this videotape is to address the increased public anxiety about nuclear energy following the Chernobyl disaster and to put the case for the economic necessity of nuclear power and for the acceptability of the levels of safety maintained by the industry in Britain.

The principal feature of the programme's communicative design is its imitation of certain aspects of broadcast television's established 'current affairs' discourses. By using Brian Walden as its presenter it is able to use the model of Thames Television's *Weekend World* (in which Walden first came to public attention as a TV personality) and to mediate its promotional appeals through the codes of impartial journalistic exposition.

The principal feature of the programme's thematic development is its extensive dependence on the recently published report of the public inquiry into the building of a Pressurised Water Reactor at Sizewell in Suffolk. This inquiry (chaired by Sir Frank Layfield and referred to in the programme by its short title 'The Layfield Report') produced findings which were generally positive about the efficiency and safety of the nuclear industry. Regular reference to these findings is made throughout the programme and the Report is used as independent corroborative support for many of the programme's own assessments.

1. Communicative Design

The programme starts in a brisk, 'newsy' style with Brian Walden noting the recent Government decision to proceed with a further stage of its nuclear energy plan, following the positive findings of the Sizewell Inquiry. By launching the programme from journalism-style headlines, this opening serves to displace the non-journalistic promotional motivations at work. Having greeted the viewer from his (familiar) studio setting, Walden can then proceed with an account framed in terms of independent current-affairs analysis developing naturally from the pre-constituted realm of the *topical*. The precise aim of this analysis is stated early on, in a manner which keeps close to the codes of impartiality by ventriloqizing the comments of those who 'harbour grave doubts' about nuclear power:

> They ask 'Why do we need these new nuclear power stations when so many other energy sources are available? Even if nuclear power is in some ways preferable to the alternatives, do the benefits really outweigh the risks?' These are the questions we'll be trying to answer in this programme.

This mode of representing alternative or conflicting views by 'voicing' them rather than by accessing the spokespersons who could give them authentic expression is one which ensures that the promotional design subsumes, and therefore is never threatened by, all of the points emerging from the 'impartial

Fig. 3. *Energy – The Nuclear Option*: Broadcast current-affairs styles imitated.

Fig. 4. *Energy – The Nuclear Option*: The Chairman under questioning.

inquiry'. The statement is also indicative of the highly explicit and often emphatic expositional spine given to the programme by Walden's comments, a further use of his established public persona as a presenter of unswerving commitment to clear and logical understanding.

The programme's subsequent development in trying to answer the central question of the relation of benefits to risks is one which is made up of shifts between commentary-over-film, graphics, 'single comment' interview snippets and a final question-and-answer interview sequence with Lord Marshall, Chairman of the CEGB. Throughout this, regular return is made to the mode of presenter direct-address from the studio, a mode which sustains a shadowing of current-affairs codes and which, through its very immediacy and directness, regulates the viewer's relationship to the terms of all other contributions.

In the final interview with Marshall, where Walden asks questions in shot, the relationship between promotional aims and journalistic forms moves to a further modality of co-existence. For the interview is essentially an exercise in persuasive theatricality, the close questioning of the interviewer being precisely designed to show the strengths of the interviewee's position. There are clearly risks attached to using this form of presentation and our later discussion of respondent comments brings these out. The questioning cannot afford to be perceived as 'too soft', otherwise both the integrity of the interviewer and the status of the responses will be greatly impaired. But nor can the questioning be 'too hard', since the risk is then of stimulating a critical alertness in the viewer against which the interviewee's task (here, of providing reassurance) is made more difficult. Unlike that use of 'ventriloquistic' speech to register doubt and counter-argument which we noted above, it is not a problem which has a readily available solution and we indicate in the following sub-section (and then in Chapter 4) how it troubles the coherence and meaning of this important, climactic sequence of the programme.

2. Thematic Development

Some of the key themes which the programme variously treats are:

(a) Alternative sources of energy and their shortcomings.

(b) The increasing need for electrical energy both in the developed and developing world (this together with an emphasis on the economic and political stability of nuclear energy sources).

(c) The difference between current British technology and the technologies involved in the Chernobyl disaster and in the Three-Mile Island incident.

(d) The very high levels of safety, both in engineered design and routine operation, maintained within the industry.

As well as film sequences, the programme is able to recruit to the development of these themes a variety of speakers (eg an academic physicist, senior management within the industry, a safety specialist, an engineer), testifying positively to the emerging conclusion of the account that the benefits exceed the risks. Walden's commentary indicates the phased move of the programme towards this verdict. Here are two examples of his 'signposting' statements, summarising phases:

> *There is no risk of a Chernobyl-type accident to set against the benefits.*

> *All the evidence suggests that the benefits outweigh the risks. The benefits are great but the risks are small.*

It is against this confidence that the programme poses the question which acts as an introduction to the Marshall interview – 'Why, then, has so much suspicion built up among the public?'. Marshall's answer is that the CEGB has been neglectful of public education and has not been as open with the public about the real (and safe) nature of nuclear processes as they should have been. This answer is followed by other reassuring comments, with the recognition that though nothing can be *entirely* guaranteed, nuclear energy is one of the safest sources of power available. A problem arises when Walden asks about possible public anxiety that a power station might explode like a nuclear bomb. Marshall rejects the naivety of this belief but, in describing Chernobyl as a worst possible case, develops a vividness of account regarding the initial damage which prompts Walden to ask whether Chernobyl wasn't, then, 'just a little bit like a bomb?'. This may appear a relatively trivial exchange, foregrounding Walden's ability to come back smartly on an answer without necessarily putting it into *substantial* question (and in any case, there is an important slippage of scale involved here, down from 'nuclear bomb' to 'bomb'). However, we shall show below how significant this exchange was within the interpretative accounts of respondents. Moreover, Marshall's reply to a final question, on the significance to be given to the occurrence of 'cancer clusters' around nuclear power stations, is, in its abrupt dismissiveness ('you find them wherever you look'), also registered negatively in a number of respondent accounts.

Nevertheless, in his final address from the studio, Walden feels the cumulative force of evidence sufficient to support a statement whose normative appeal brings the programme to an end:

> *It can't be guaranteed that nothing will ever go wrong, of course. Life's not like that. It can be reasonably argued that the nuclear power industry can be regarded in the same way as any other complex technology, and recognised as a normal and necessary part of our daily lives and not like some mysterious monster to fill us with irrational dread.*

From Our Own Correspondent (Northern Newsreel Number 9, Trade Films).

The dramatic narrative which forms the basis of this item's communicative design, about an imaginary disaster at Hartlepool Power Station, seeks to involve the viewer very directly with the personal consequences of such a disaster for one, typical, family. Thematically, it touches upon such matters as plant safety, emergency planning, the health risks of radiation exposure, practical provision and compensation for victims. Emergency planning is the most salient of these themes. Both communicative design and thematic development take the Chernobyl disaster as a point of reference. The communicative strategy of the piece depends upon a ploy to make viewers initially 'misunderstand' that it is about the Russian disaster when in fact it is about Hartlepool in England as seen and interpreted on Soviet television. Thematically, the point of the exercise is the analogy with Chernobyl, projected with particular regard to the effects upon the local population.

1. Communicative design

Dramatisation is used in the piece not to re-present a past event, or typify a current situation, as in much mainstream drama-documentary, but to create an imaginary past and an imaginary present. The imaginary present is a Soviet news studio: from this reference point is constructed an account of the imaginary past – the Hartlepool disaster, worse than Chernobyl itself.

From Our Own Correspondent was made and distributed two years after the Soviet Union's *real* nuclear disaster. It reverses the 'them' and 'us' relations that would be involved in doing a Chernobyl story on British television in 1988. But it is of crucial significance that this fictive scenario is confirmed only *after* an initial sequence which is naturally interpreted as the introduction to a Chernobyl story. This interpretation is encouraged (a) by using footage from Chernobyl in the opening sequence, (b) by making Russia the primary frame, thereby implicating 'Russian affairs', (c) by referring to 'the world's most serious nuclear accident' – an unambiguous expression in the real world of 1988.

Even the communicative relations of the item – a Russian programme for Russian viewers – are constructed in the terms of the fiction. As the item begins we see shots of disaster accompanied by untranslated Russian voiceover. These are followed by a shot from a news studio. The male news reader's direct address is also in Russian. An English voiceover translation constructs British viewers as secondary recipients. Then there begins a film sequence from Britain, narrated by a female Russian reporter, notionally 'translated' into English (her Russian voice is faded out after a few seconds). It is she who controverts our confident interpretation of this as a Chernobyl story:

Fig. 5. *From Our Own Correspondent*: A Soviet journalist from the 'contaminated zone' around Hartlepool nuclear power station, two years after the 'world's most serious nuclear accident'.
Fig. 6. *From Our Own Correspondent*: The human face of nuclear catastrophe: interview with the mother of a sick child.

The scene here is calm, almost tranquil. It's hard to recall now the panic, the chaos and the tragedy of that day exactly two years ago when this peaceful countryside was shattered by an explosion less than fifteen kilometers from here in the nuclear power station at Hartlepool.

Another shift then takes us back to the time of the disaster, focussing on the evacuation and including the first of two interview sequences with 'Susan Duffy', an evacuee. This episode is linked with a subsequent one on 'Hartlepool now' – the bridge between the two is an on-screen piece to camera by the reporter.

Any facts about the British situation which emerge during this narration always do so within the fictional frame, which qualifies their 'facticity'. Only right at the end does the item adopt a 'reality' framing in which there has as yet been no major disaster at Hartlepool. The different status of this discourse is signalled formally – instead of voices we get captions over a frozen shot of Hartlepool power station. This sequence gives brief details of a recent accident there which caused a breakdown of the cooling mechanism, and compares Hartlepool's one kilometer evacuation zone with evacuation zones of up to 16 kilometers in other Western countries. Our experience with viewers suggests that the relations of address involved in this text present a considerable challenge to their interpretative abilities and that they are not invariably successful in negotiating its frame-shifts (See Chapter 5 for further discussion of this point).

2. Thematic development

There is no attempt to construct a propositional account in justification of the hypothesis which underlies the drama, that a Chernobyl-scale disaster is possible in Britain. The possibility of such a disaster is, of course, consistently denied by the industry, often citing Russian scientific opinion as support. The scenario is offered as plausible in this text by using the example of Chernobyl to suggest that *official* reassurance should itself be treated as grounds for suspicion – after all, the Russian authorities used to deny that there could be a major disaster in *their* country. This reasoning is implicit in the structure of the text, and made explicit in the closing captions:

According to the CEGB the events depicted in this film could never happen in Britain.

The Russians said the same before Chernobyl.

Critical conclusions about the industry are drawn as if from hindsight. Thus Susan Duffy and her family have to wait 48 hours before they are evacuated because no proper evacuation plans exist(ed) except for a tiny number of people within a one kilometre radius of the plant. Two years later, still in temporary accommodation, and with her son suffering from leukaemia, it transpires that no compensation has been paid to the family because the government and the industry are fighting over the question of responsibility. The news story framework also allows the introduction of broader, non-experiential themes, as when the narrator refers to 'the controversial decision to allow some of these plants to be privately owned' as a contributory factor (a decision since reversed by the government).

3. Visualisation

The format of the item allows considerable scope for evoking mood through imagery. The disaster's initial chaos is depicted in the evacuation scene. We get a night-time sequence of the Duffy family and others rushing out of their homes and into coaches; dark shots of traffic jams, and an interview with Susan Duffy in the back of the coach, when the reporter finds out how little they know about what's going on. The tragic effects on people and communities are also conveyed through particular, single shots of, for instance, deserted beaches, an abandoned doll, and family photographs on the mantlepiece of an uninhabitable home.

When the reporter herself appears on screen, to bring viewers up to date two years after the event, her red beret and red microphone project her foreignness in almost stereotypical terms. She is depicted walking along by the intimidating wire fence which surrounds the danger zone around the plant itself, still hazardous after all this time. This fence, and a wasteland beyond, is all we are allowed to see. The images here symbolise rather than depict the plant and the disaster.

The fictionalisation and dramatization of disaster in terms of its human consequences uses these two kinds of affective imagery as part of its attempt to draw viewers into a directly emotional response. An involvement with personal circumstances is generated by the urgency of naturalistic news-style depiction, but other images have a deeper symbolic force, suggesting a tragedy, pathos, destruction and decay which go beyond the individual circumstances of the Duffy family to the whole community and landscape.

Heart of the Matter (BBC2)

Heart of the Matter is an established BBC series, scheduled for late-night Sunday transmission on BBC1. As its title suggests, the series seeks to establish the central points at issue in each 'matter' treated and to clarify them in the interests of wider public understanding. This it does by the use of a presenter/reporter, location filming and the testimony and comment of people directly involved in the issues as well as contributions from relevant official bodies and individual specialists. As its title also suggests, and as its Sunday scheduling might indicate too, it is particularly concerned to register the 'human' dimension of the problems and dilemmas it investigates.

The edition of the programme which we examined (broadcast on 18th June 1989) was entitled 'A Life Or A Living?' and concerned itself with the decision by a number of parents living in the Sellafield area to sue BNFL for damages in respect of their children's leukaemia. The programme focuses on one such parent, Mrs Sue D'Arcy of Cleator Moor, who is proceeding with a case on behalf of her daughter Gemma, recently diagnosed as suffering from acute mycelic leukaemia. (Mr D'Arcy, an employee at the Sellafield plant, does not support this action and has refused to be filmed or interviewed).

1. Communicative Design

Around this family tragedy and its consequent, internal tensions the programme builds a more broadly-conceived account of the Sellafield-leukaemia connection, its history and the current factors in play, scientifically and legally. It does this principally by interviews with five main participants, who are returned to a number of times and whose comments and counter-comments provide the main programme content. These speakers are Mrs D'Arcy herself; her solicitor; the local GP; a radiation specialist and a representative of BNFL. In addition, there is a substantial and important contribution to the last half of the programme by Professor Sir Richard Doll, the research scientist who was a leading figure in the discovery of the link between cigarette smoking and lung cancer. The programme's progression through the interviews is aided both by commentary and a number of pieces-to-camera from the presenter, Joan Bakewell, and by supportive film of family activities, the local landscape, key documents referred to and various features of the Sellafield plant.

Although, when compared to the other programmes we have analysed, this one is rhetorically quite restrained, both visually and verbally, it nevertheless opens with one of the most widely used tropes in televised depictions of Sellafield – the contrast between the beauty of the natural landscape and the highly un-natural threat potentially posed by the nuclear industry located within it. This contrast is also one between the world of appearance and the world of (possible) reality, as we discuss in Chapter 3. Over shots of a lake, sparkling under a clear, summer sky and set within a landscape of mountains, woods and fields, Bakewell launches the programme with this comment:

> *The beautiful countryside of the Lake District. What a wonderful place to live and bring up children. Most of us cherish an idyllic vision of the countryside and this comes as close to it as any. The natural life, the good life. Well, that's how it looks.*

With the dynamics of doubt thus released into the programme through an ironic turn at its very beginning, the introduction then shifts tone to outline the details behind that marked note of reservation. Moving on from lakeside beauty to a more general shot of the landscape, and locating within this a distant view of the Sellafield site, the connection with jobs and industry is developed. The arrival of the nuclear energy research station in the late 1940s brought a radical improvement in job prospects. But, the commentary tells us, it also brought something else – an increasingly unignorable threat of health damage following exposure to increased levels of radiation. This threat is most dramatically manifest in the high incidence (10 times the national average) of childhood leukaemia among those communities in the vicinity of the plant. Here, then, the programme finds its focus, together with the resulting dilemma it poses for individuals living and working in the area:

> What lies at the heart of the matter is how to weigh the value of the industry to the community against their fears for the health of their children.

Having established a frame, the programme gives the viewer a preliminary glimpse of its main speakers and (through tightly edited interview 'snippets') a sense of the inter-related and conflicting positions they will develop later. The pace of the programme then eases from directly propositional address to offer a more sustained and experientially-grounded treatment of the D'Arcy case. This involves the interview testimony of Mrs D'Arcy and some 'relaxed' observational filming of mother and daughter at home, having tea with the presenter in their garden. That *this* level of 'the matter' and of attempts to resolve it has its own immediate and highly personal character is pointed-up by the commentary:

> For them, it isn't simply a matter of cold, scientific facts. It's the outcome of continuing and bitter experience, of worry, outrage, of pain and the most appalling realisation any parent can come to.

The central and longest phase of the programme follows, pulling back from the immediately personal to a more general consideration of the case in its context, during which the five central participants develop the main themes at issue. This is done largely through a sequence of location interviews, sometimes intercut with more general informational shots. For instance, a shot of the beach at Seascale, the beach on which Gemma D'Arcy played, is accompanied by the voice of her mother reflecting on the dangers which 'each stone' might have carried for her daughter's health. The shot of the deserted expanse develops, in context, a disquieting symbolism in addition to its denotative function. The ties in with a challenge about the *reasons* for its being deserted, made by Bakewell to the BNFL spokesman in the course of an interview.

At the end of the sequence of contextualizing interviews, the programme pulls back even further to consider briefly some of the general statistical and ethical questions surrounding calculations of benefit and risk ('brutal equations') in industrial society. Finally, however, as we note below, it narrows sharply down again in order to connect with the particular and the experiential in articulating a conclusion.

2. Thematic Development

This occurs principally in the central section of the programme and might be itemised as having five main strands:

(a) The story of the legal initiative, including BNFL's representation to the Law Society that Legal Aid should not be claimable by litigants. The programme traces the origins of this initiative in the publication of a report by the Committee on Medical Aspects of Radiation in the Environment (COMARE). This committee surveyed the Sellafield area in 1986 and, two years later in remarks covering the whole of its findings, it noted that:

> *Evidence of abnormal incidence of leukaemia tends to support the hypothesis that some feature of the nuclear plants that we have examined leads to an increased risk of leukaemia in young people living in the vicinity.*[7]

(b) The attitudes of the local community towards, on the one hand, the, economic benefits of the Sellafield site and BNFL's continued support for local recreational and leisure facilities and, on the other, towards the perceived risks the operations have brought to the area. This dependency/risk relationship, identified early on, is developed as the central dilemma .

(c) The scientific factors involved in making the link between Sellafield, radiation and leukaemia. The matters of proof and of disproof involved and the current state of scientific opinion both on this and on the question of the acceptable exposure-levels used as guidelines in the industry are explored and debated.

(d) BNFL's perspective on the question, in terms of plant safety, monitoring procedures, public information and the recent use of high profile publicity through the activities of the Sellafield Visitor's Centre and related national advertising campaigns (from which the latest television commercial is shown). The history of the site as a place which has previously attracted a *mis*placed confidence in its safety is briefly but pointedly 'remembered' by the programme, particularly the 1957 Windscale fire, which is now calculated to have lead to 33 deaths, though at the time no long-term health damage was thought to have occurred.

(e) The contrast between the scientific and legal criteria for establishing causality ('Science is one thing, Law is another' says the commentary). Even within the legal system there are important differences. Liability in a Civil Court requires only that a 'balance of probability' be found to exist, not (as in the case of criminal proceedings) that the case be proved 'beyond all reasonable doubt'.

The programme ends its treatments of the issues – personal, legal,scientific and industrial – by remarking on the two different levels of consequence which might

---

7 *This quotation from the COMARE report was cited during the course of the programme.*

follow from the impending court action which is 'about to make history'. There are the immediate consequences for the D'Arcy family and the other families seeking compensation, and then there are the broader consequences for the nuclear industry's own perspectives on 'risk levels', for its research priorities and processing methods and, most important of all, for public perceptions of the acceptable benefit/risk equations within which it can be allowed to operate. At the most general level reached by the programme, the acceptability of such equations is seen to be informed by a sense of the *inevitability* of a certain level of risk in all industrial processes. However, this level of formulation, referencing the ultimate parameters, does not have an *immediate* bearing on the coming court case and what might follow. The programme therefore concludes by tightening-up once more around its principal human focus – Gemma D'Arcy smiling in her paddling pool, first in action and then in freeze-frame:

> *Meanwhile Gemma D'Arcy waits for a possible bone marrow transplant, that could save her life and the search goes on for a way to avoid more leukaemias.*

A Note On Production Backgrounds

In order to connect some of the points made in these commentaries with matters of producer intentions and production contexts, we briefly indicate below those significant aspects of production which we have been able to discover through documentation and interview concerning our three Phase One programmes.

1. Uncertain Legacy

In 1986, a decision to undertake a series of programmes on nuclear energy was initiated by the Features and Documentaries department at BBC Manchester.[8] Although the recency of the Chernobyl disaster was undoubtedly a factor in this decision, the immediate and more central motivation for it was the feeling that the nuclear industry in Britain was at a turning point and that its future very much depended on the state of public opinion. This gave the team a guiding principle for the series 'Taming the Dragon', to examine the basis upon which the government at that time (with Peter Walker as the relevant minister) proposed to expand the nuclear industry and, specifically, to introduce pressurised water reactors into Britain. A speech by Peter Walker was used as the reference point – he had claimed that nuclear power was clean, cheap and safe compared with other means of producing electricity. The three part series which was eventually broadcast took each of these claims and subjected them to critical inquiry. Thus *Uncertain Legacy* was intended as a challenge by the team to the presumption of safety which the Government as well as the industry appeared to have made.

---

8 *Information in this section is based upon an interview with the producer, Peter Dale.*

This was a programme which, to be effective, required the co-operation of the industry for obtaining film footage and interviews with key personnel. Although this co-operation was readily obtained, presumably from the mixed motives of obligation and self-interest, the reaction to the finished product was unfavourable, and the director was attacked as dishonest. Two articles by David Taylor, based upon the series, were published in *The Listener*. They were followed by critical responses in the Letters pages. Correspondents included spokesmen for the Atomic Energy Authority, the CEGB and the Nuclear Energy Information Group.[9]

All three programmes attracted a very small audience – around one million – by the standards of the *Brass Tacks* slot into which they were placed as a 'special'. Nevertheless, they got a very high appreciation rating from the audience (74 per cent). The team were very much aware that they would be challenged on grounds of bias but were prepared to defend a 'civic' role in terms of the need for a public critique of propositions, for instance, those concerning safety, which had been accepted by the government in spite of their tendentiousness. Another justification was that they had introduced crucial new information into the public debate. In the case of *Uncertain Legacy*, the most relevant new information as the team perceived it was the medical research from Hiroshima. New cancers there suggested people were at risk at lower levels of exposure than had been previously thought.

The team were also conscious of setting up counter-images to those of the industry: if the latter was prepared to offer patronising and blandly uninformative analogies of minimal risk – exposure to radiation in Sellafield is like 'smoking one cigarette in your lifetime' – then the programme was prepared to present a number of disturbing visual images of maximal risk, as we discuss below.

2. Energy – The Nuclear Option

This half-hour video was made for the Central Electricity Generating Board by Software Productions Ltd. and distributed by the CEGB's film and video library for either hire or purchase from late 1987. A leaflet was mailed to 30,000 possibly interested individuals, institutions and groups (half of them named academics in U.K Higher Education). This was finally judged to be more successful in circulat-

9 *All of the following appeared in* The Listener: *David Taylor 'Cheaper energy from nuclear power was always a myth' 15 October 1987 pp 5-6; David Taylor 'Radiation risks: any limit may be too high' 22 October 1987 pp 12-13; David Lowry, 'Letters to the Editor' 29 November 1987 p 21; Peter Vey, Director of Information and Public Affairs, CEGB, 'Letters to the Editor' 12 November 1987 p 26; PAH Saunders, Head, Environmental Impact Assessments, United Kingdom Atomic Energy Authority, 'Letters to the Editor' 12 November 1987 p 26; TA Margerison, Director, Nuclear Electricity Information Group, 'Letters to the Editor' 19 November 1987 p 24; David Taylor 'Letters to the Editor', 26 November 1987 p 26; Marshall of Goring (Lord Walter Marshall) 'Letters to the Editor' 10 December 1987 p 21.*

ing the video than the press advertising, which concentrated on the quality weeklies.

The Film and Video Branch of the CEGB was responsible for the making of a number of promotional videos during the 1980s but, as leaked documents clearly show,[10] its role became of greatly heightened significance following the Chernobyl disaster in 1986. The attempt to win back public confidence in nuclear energy became at this time a priority within the CEGB and an intensified strategy of persuasion was initiated.

Energy – The Nuclear Option was regarded by the CEGB as a 'pro-active' piece of promotion, complementing some of the 'reactive' material quickly made and distributed following the Chernobyl events. It was made from a detailed script plan prepared by Software Productions and approved by the CEGB.[11] The CEGB subsequently dealt with the arrangements for shooting on various nuclear sites and were consulted throughout post-production. As in most other videos commissioned by the Board,there was some re-use of material from earlier projects.

The decision to use the TV broadcaster and ex-Labour MP Brian Walden as the presenter/interviewer was grounded in a desire to give the video a more independent character and to allow for a degree of convincingly adversarial questioning within the expositional format. The success of his London Weekend Television series *Weekend World* in handling controversial topics with a distinctive, clarifying zeal and a tone of hard inquiry was influential here. The thrust of the video was to appear investigatory, as is clear from this extract from the advertising copy prepared for release in Autumn 1987:

> *In this new 29 minute programme, ex-politician and TV presenter Brian Walden asks the questions 'Why do we need nuclear power when there are so many other energy sources available?'. 'How safe are our nuclear power stations?' and 'Do the benefits of nuclear energy really outweigh the risks?'.*

The decision to feature Lord Marshall, Chairman of the CEGB, as the main interviewee, was a simple consequence of the high-profile publicity role which he had already been performing, both in CEGB material and in broadcast and press coverage of the energy question. Although we note below some problems with viewer response both to the content and style of his contribution, percep-

---

10 *Documents leaked to* The Guardian *in June 1989 revealed how, after, Chernobyl, the CEGB rapidly set about devising a strategy of response to public anxiety. See especially* The Guardian *'Chernobyl fallout sparked PR crisis', 1 June 1989 p 9.*

11 *We are grateful for the helpful (and otherwise unobtainable), information about the tape's production background given to us during an interview in Spring 1989 by members of what was then the Film and Video Branch of the CEGB's Department of Information and Public Affairs. This included photocopies of the CEGB's own data on the distribution and effectiveness of the material.*

tions within the Board at the time were that he was a successful communicator of the nuclear message, with a good projection of personal qualities.

CEGB statistics show that approximately 60% of the distribution was to colleges and schools. A sample study suggested that almost half of the viewers of the tape watched it in groups of over 20 people, with half of the total viewers being in the 16-18 age range.

3. *From Our Own Correspondent* (Northern Newsreel 9)

The possibility of doing this video item as a dramatised scenario, playing off established public images and knowledge of Chernobyl, came to the attention of the producer and editor (both of Trade Films of Gateshead) following an advertisement appealing for scriptwriters to contribute to Northern Newsreel.[12] A script was submitted by a writer who had written previously on nuclear issues. His idea of tackling the question of a regional issue (safety at Hartlepool Nuclear Power Station) by drawing on this international imagery was immediately seen as appropriate and manageable within Northern Newsreel's resources. Details of the 'safety' debate itself and, particularly, on the contingency planning zones around the Hartlepool plant, were based heavily on a programme in the BBC *Horizon* series transmitted in 1987. This had focussed on plant design and ongoing operating problems at Hartlepool and had begun by entertaining a 'could it happen here?' hypothesis, using film of a training exercise. As in *From Our Own Correspondent*, the dramatic impact is strengthened and the significance widened by flashbacks to Chernobyl at the time of the accident and afterwards – with images of deserted streets and houses. Unlike the BBC programme, however, the aims of the video makers were to make a direct intervention into the debate by giving the 'British disaster' hypothesis an intensive and uncritical projection.

The entire shoot was completed in three days in and around Hartlepool, using only two actresses. Production emphasis was on economy of time and money and the maximum of 'awareness-raising' in the finished text, necessarily only one item among others in the edition of the Newsreel for which it was planned. Dramatic simulation of a news type format was considered acceptable financially and was central to the principal idea of the treatment – a shock twist whereby viewers start off as 'us' looking at 'them' (Soviet television coverage of Chernobyl) only to find out that really 'they' (Soviet TV) are looking at 'us' (the imagined Hartlepool disaster). An imitation of Soviet TV style also allowed freedom for a number of overtly symbolic, impressionistic visual sequences accompanied by music specially commissioned for the piece (this too was influenced by the *Horizon* film). Music was considered important by both producer and editor for mood creation.

---

12 *Information in this section is based upon an interview with the production team at Trade Films.*

Northern Newsreel see part of their role being the exploration of alternative styles, largely to avoid imitating broadcast television. The producer and director of *From Our Own Correspondent* sought primarily an *emotional* impact and response because such a response was seen by them to be the prerequisite to a rational debate : 'A rational discussion of nuclear energy demands emotional commitment'.

 The jump from Chernobyl to Hartlepool (actually a jump only in where viewers *think* they are) was considered unproblematic by the programme-makers, who intended 'to string people along as far as possible'. They noted that if, with some viewers, such a strategy led to temporary ambiguity over whether the accident did or didn't happen, this would be all the better as it would add to the drama and increase involvement. However, the producer had reservations about the final sequence, which moves out from the fictional scenario to the real circumstances at Hartlepool at the time, using captions over a still frame. His anxieties, confirmed by our research as shown below and in Chapter 4, were that such a very late shift to an exposition of the real, current situation, involving a change in discursive methods, might either 'throw' viewers or simply go unregistered in the wake of the emotional force of the dramatisation.

3 Four key themes

In Chapter 2 we gave a descriptive account of the four texts used in this study. The present chapter complements those accounts by looking at the programmes from a more comparative perspective. Four themes seemed to us worthy of discussion across the selected texts. Under the heading *Proof and probability* we consider how the programmes connect with scientific discussions of causation in the nuclear debate. *Experts and ordinary people* looks at the types and degrees of credibility accorded to different accessed voices. *The imagery of threat* emphasises the visual imagery of the texts with particular reference to associational meanings. Finally, *Lessons from the past* discusses the thematization of key events from the history of the nuclear industry. Although both substantive and formal considerations inform each section, the emphasis varies, so that, for instance, the discussion in *Proof and probability* has a primarily substantive focus whilst *Experts and ordinary people* shows more interest in forms.

Proof and probability

You can't prove a scientific theory when you're trying to look at cause and effect

These are the words of Robin Russell Jones, editor of *Radiation and Health*, the radiation expert who comments on the Sellafield leukaemia prosecution in *Heart of the Matter* '(Un)provability' is a thematic concern of all of the programmes, from the question of what caused one child's leukaemia at the lowest level of generality through to philosophical reflection on the nature of proof at the highest, taking in the difference between legal (civil and criminal) and scientific standards of proof. If anything is central to the nuclear risk debate it is this 'proof' issue. The discourse of this debate, as conducted in the public sphere and mediated by television, poses questions both of the past 'Has anyone been made ill or killed by the industry?' and of the future 'Will there be a nuclear accident in Britain and what will be its effects if there is?' With regard to the first, conclusive 'proof' would require watertight epidemiological axioms and a closed causal narrative (one from which alternative explanations of individual or collective suffering have been eliminated). These are impossible conditions, so the actual choice is between 'talking up' an effects scenario, maximally into probability so convincing it amounts to proof, or talking it 'down' into mere possibility, improbability or even impossibility. Future danger, as envisaged in *From Our Own Correspondent*, is an even more speculative matter. Of course, possibility/probability is not *just* a matter of rhetoric: it is rational, other things being equal, to find certain kinds of evidence and argument more persuasive than others in respect of a given 'unknown'.

Both those who criticise the nuclear power industry and those who seek to reassure the fearful support their positions by appeal to rationality and scientific evidence. Their arguments are variously mediated in the texts we have used for this study. No programme addresses its viewers directly in the discourses of chemistry, physics or epidemiology (or allows its expert witnesses to do so); if necessary the language of the experts is translated for the viewers or explained to them. *Uncertain Legacy* introduces the concept of a 'millisievert'. *Energy – the Nuclear Option* explains the construction principles of a PWR with particular emphasis upon safety features. *Heart of the Matter* expounds, as an alternative to the account of Sellafield leukaemias as radiation-induced illnesses, an 'infection' theory of how such an excessive leukaemia rate might have come about. Only *From Our Own Correspondent*, with its 'what if...?' approach, stays at a distance from the scientific-empirical.

The programmes, particularly the broadcast ones (*Uncertain Legacy*, *Heart of the Matter*) which we shall concentrate upon here, all appeal to the rationality of the viewers themselves, as competent to make certain kinds of judgements on the basis of the evidence presented, even where, as in *Uncertain Legacy*, the inconclusiveness of even its own evidence is signalled. The presenter takes the viewers through a 'case study' in the Somerset County Records office, showing an increase in the numbers of infant deaths associated with congenital malformations, during a three year period which is also a 'peak' for leukaemia cases in the same area. This is the logic of 'telling coincidence', which the presenter invokes in detached terms, stressing the importance of cross-referencing statistical findings. Nevertheless, he concludes:

> But of course you can prove anything with statistics. And whilst these figures strengthen the argument that we're dealing with radiation induced disease, they do no more than that. There is no smoking gun, no evidence of Hinkley Point's involvement. But clearly something happened here in Somerset in the late 60s for which there is no obvious explanation.

There is no smoking gun because the industry's own records do not show a significant increase in radiation emission for the relevant period. Viewers are allowed, rather than encouraged, to speculate that independent records on radiation emission might have shown something different: 'we have to take the industry's word for it', Taylor says – and, for the purposes of the argument on hand, he does.

One very strong card that *Uncertain Legacy* plays, to strengthen its credibility of argument, is the challenging of those epidemiological axioms which have underpinned the discussion about radiation-induced disease. This card is a telling one as played within the programme's textualization of the nuclear power debate. It is of additional interest to us inasmuch as the validity of these axioms is again raised as an issue, but less conclusively, in *Heart of the Matter*. The axioms in question are, we learn, derived from data on the victims of the Hiroshima/Nagasaki atom bombs. They are thus above suspicion, in one sense – medical research has no interest in making the effects of the A-bombs seem better or worse than they are. Sir Douglas Black, in producing his report, thus relied just as much upon these axioms as did the industry in setting its maximum permissible dose limits. In doing so, Black came to the 'paradoxical' conclusion that Sellafield had emitted too little radiation to be responsible for the excessive cancer rate in the area. *Uncertain Lecacy's* card is this – on the basis of the latest data from Japan *medical research has changed its mind*; the axioms need revision:

> There has been a disproportionately high number of cancer deaths among the 15,000 Hiroshima and Nagasaki citizens who received comparatively small amounts of radiation. An average internal tissue dose of 103 millisieverts. Now if current radiation risk estimates are correct there should be no more than 20 excess cancers within this group but actually there's been over 100. Which suggests that our dose limits could be at least 5 times too high.

The presenter goes on to argue that dose limits could in fact be ten times too high, with support from John Goffman, an eminent American scientist. We discuss below the functions of expert, as against lay testimony in these programmes. Here it is sufficient to point out that viewers' rationality can be exercised in judging the credibility of evidence *sources* rather than in judging the evidence itself – the assumption being that only an expert could do the latter – with more or less assistance from within the text. In *Energy – The Nuclear Option* the trustworthiness of Sir Frank Layfield's testimony, the Layfield Report, that PWR's are a safe form of electricity generation, is not directly argued for but implicitly rests upon the impartiality of the inquiry process itself. By contrast, when *From Our Own Correspondent* seeks to discredit the reassuring testimony of official sources that a Chernobyl-type disaster is impossible in Britain, a rationale for scepticism is made more explicit. The Chernobyl accident happened although the authorities said it couldn't. So the British authorities could be wrong too.

But a rational approach, to evidence or to sources, is not enough to yield uncontestable truths in the nuclear power debate. This ultimate indeterminacy is most directly confronted in *Heart of the Matter*. An industry spokesman puts the view (with some support from Joan Bakewell) that a legal verdict (produced by a judge, or by a jury) is a different matter from a scientific fact (produced by a scientist or scientific community). The solicitor for the afflicted Sellafield family, hopeful of a verdict favouring his clients, admits that such a verdict is the more likely given that this is a civil case, where the standard of proof is the 'balance of probabilities' rather than 'beyond all reasonable doubt', as in the case of a criminal trial. Russell Jones, the programme's radiation expert, generalizes 'unprovability' to *all* scientific claims – he is nevertheless emphatic on the subject of the industry's responsibility, and his rhetorical strategy would seem to involve an attempt to shift the burden of proof from the litigants to the defendants:

> *You can't prove a scientific theory when you're trying to look at cause and effect. All you can do, in the words of Karl Popper, is to disprove it. In other words you have to find some item of data which actually disproves the link between the discharges and the leukaemia. And this was something that really has been misunderstood from the very beginning, people have expected science to provide proof. It is not in the nature of science to provide proof. It is in the nature of science to disprove things.*

In taking a line against the industry, the critics in this programme offer BNFL two options: to fight the case but accept the burden of proof on epistemological grounds (Russell Jones' position) or not to fight the case and admit liability on moral grounds – the position of the local GP:

> *I think they should morally accept that connection whether it's out of court or in court, I don't think it matters. But I think it's been the attitude all the way along that BNFL won't accept a connection and while that happens it makes me very angry.*

It is a reasonable position to take – and seems to be Russell Jones' premise – that since conclusive proof is not possible, probability has to be enough, for the law and for science. This is undoubtedly true insofar as science relies on statistical methods which are inherently probabilistic. On this reasoning it would be dishonourable for the industry to hold out for conclusiveness before they will admit liability. For they too must know, from their own scientific experts, that this is not possible.

In fact the industry comes across in the programme rather better than this (implicit) line of argument suggests: for the industry spokesman the litigants case rests on *improbable* facts, not on *unproven* ones in the hard sense, although his own position appears to rely upon the same epidemiological axioms as were challenged in *Uncertain Legacy*:

> *If the accusation is that the cause is radioactivity and radiation from Sellafield we just do not consider that that is possible. All the scientifically accepted relationships between dose and risk would have to be wrong, and not just wrong but wrong by several orders of magnitude for this to be the case.*

An independent scientist, Sir Richard Doll, makes the same point – radiation could not have been the cause of the leukaemia cluster in this case. The industry spokesman and Doll also agree – the former more grudgingly – that some other aspect of the plant's operation could be responsible. The picture that emerges is of a genuine scientific problem in explaining particular leukaemia clusters. At its weakest, the case against the industry as mediated to the viewer in this programme relies upon the mere possibility of a causal relationship based upon the co-occurrence of radiation emission and excess leukaemia cases. That co-occurrence is most emphatically stated from the very beginning and is one of the things that is, as Bakewell explicitly establishes, beyond dispute for all parties. The emphatic tones with which the 'facts' are stated by Russell Jones (that Sellafield emits radiation; that there is a leukaemia cluster in the area) do not lead on to an equally emphatic content at this point: the best he can come up with is 'plausibility' for the causal connection:

> So in the context of Sellafield the thesis is that the discharges are responsible for the radiation (sic). Now that is a perfectly plausible biological statement.

Russell Jones would, indeed, revise the 'scientifically accepted relationships between dose and risk', using evidence from Sellafield as part of the basis for revision. By the end of the programme the industry's liability remains unproven either way, though a scenario in which it is liable, but not through radiation discharges, is emerging as a strong contender. However, as we have noted earlier, it is a scenario of judgment in the *judicial*, not the *scientific* context which dominates the closing phase of this programme.

Experts and Ordinary People

The documentaries we examined used 'accessed voice' in a variety of ways within their accounts. By 'accessed voice' we refer to speech which is not that of broadcasting professionals. The most obvious form in which this occurs is the location interview, but there are considerable variations – interviewer seen/unseen, interviewer heard/unheard, interviewee fully established in setting or held in close-up, etc – all of which may modify the relations between 'accessed speaker' and viewers. A major division in the *kind* of speakers used is that between 'experts' and 'ordinary people'. This distinction holds good for a wide range of documentary programming but it is particularly true of those programme where highly technical matters lie at the centre of the debate. Here, the principal speaking role of the 'experts' is that of authoritatively mediating knowledge, whereas the role of 'ordinary people' is usually that of recounting experience. This does not, however, lead to a situation in which expertise is *inevitably* placed superior to ordinary apprehension (and perhaps anxiety). First of all, it is possible for a programme to indicate the *conflict* of opinion which exists among experts.

So, for instance, in *Uncertain Legacy*, the use of the critical testimony of American scientist and former employee of the U.S. nuclear industry John Goffman, serves to problematize the flow of official, reassuring explanations. At points, conflicting judgements are given a 'shock' juxtaposition by inter-cutting. In *Heart of the Matter*, to take another instance, an expert in radiation offers an account of dose-levels and risk factors of a far more worrying kind than that presented moments earlier by a BNFL spokesman.

Secondly, far from presenting lay testimony and suspicion as something to be read within an outer frame provided by authoritative specialist knowledge, a programme may use 'ordinary' accounts to apply sceptical pressure to aspects of expertise. This latter may thus be projected as a vulnerable 'in theory' to which lay accounts of 'in practice' can be vigorously counterposed. An implicit antagonism of this kind occurs in *Uncertain Legacy* and it is interesting to note how it is indicated by the presenter, very early in the programme, projecting significant pronominal alignments:

> *We were all innocent once. When the CEGB built Hinkley Point we believed in the nuclear dream. Now, for many of us, it's become something to protest about.*

In addition to the possibilities of inter-expert disagreement and of a programme itself being rhetorically organised from a markedly sceptical position, the extent to which given experts are perceived as *speaking for the industry* (and therefore as potentially compromised in their scientific impartiality) also needs to be addressed. It is, of course, a key factor in determining the degree of viewer-perceived conflict between expert and lay positions. *Energy – The Nuclear Option* raises this question most obviously, since all the expert speakers here (both scientific and technological) have volunteered to contribute their testimony within its essentially promotional design. Their discourse of objective professionalism is thus potentially compromised by readings of them as interested parties (as we document below in our respondent studies). This is especially so when the programme context for their speech excludes inter-expert debate and represents 'ordinary people' only by narrator projections of the 'typical' forms their fears and objections might take.

It might now be useful to review briefly the discursive sub-systems formed by different accessed voices in each of the four programmes we took for close analysis, drawing on and developing the points already made above.

As we have noted, the overall design of *Uncertain Legacy* is one which features inter-expert disagreement and which also counterposes 'ordinary' anxieties to the explanations of the industry's specialists. The narrator is able to use 'we' and 'us' very early in the programme, a signal of its intention to place one particular 'they' firmly under critical scrutiny. When, for instance, a Welsh farmer or Cumbrian mothers express their anxieties, these serve to develop and reinforce the movement of the narration and imagery (see above). There is even evidence of the narration amplifying, if not actually distorting, the level of popular anxiety. When Cumbrian families are seen undergoing voluntary body-scan testing, one woman explains that it is to 'reassure' relatives in another part of the country that 'everything is all right'. Yet the narrator generalises above this instance to remark on the 'inner fears' of the local population. In *Uncertain Legacy*, then, the expert discourse of the industry, embedded as it is within an imagery of threat and an ironic narrator framing, is matched not only against counter-expertise but against a lay testimony of considerable cumulative power.

Such an 'imbalance' is precisely reversed in *Energy – The Nuclear Option*, where the strong projection of expert reassurance is the key rhetorical aim. Given the nature of this programme as a promotional video, 'imbalance' might be a misleading term to use. Nevertheless, the total exclusion of an 'ordinary' perspective from the account, except via the ventriloquistic projections of the narrator, runs the risk of failing to *engage* properly with anxiety in the public/audience before putting the case for its unfoundedness. Possible consequences of this – condescension of tone and a suggestion that the public is almost culpably prone to superstition – were detected in the programme by many of our respondents, as we document below.

From Our Own Correspondent is, from the start, constructed in such a way as to foreground 'ordinary people' as victims of governmental and industrial negligence. This is not only established visually, through the disaster scenario of evacuation and temporary accomodation in camps, but also through the two interviews with one such victim – a mother. In the second of these interviews, she identifies the 'popular' position which the whole item is designed to project:

> *British Electricity and the Government, they just refuse to accept any responsibility. They're batting the blame between the two of them and meanwhile it's us in the middle who have to suffer.*

Finally, what distinguishes *Heart of the Matter* from the other programmes is a configuration which places the case of an 'ordinary' family right at the centre of concern, then draws back to an 'outer' ring of conflicting expert comment in an attempt at a more general understanding. This split-level approach reduces the more directly antagonistic expert-lay relations which we have noted elsewhere, a reduction which is further aided by the presentation of the family's case through the professional offices of a local lawyer. It is clear from respondent comment, however, that it is the sustained treatment of the *experience* of 'ordinary' suffering which provides the primary line of viewer engagement throughout.

The Imagery of Threat

Within the discursive repertoire which television brings to the treatment of the nuclear energy issue, there clearly exist possibilities for triggering evaluations and moods in the viewer in a manner which is both extra-rational and implicit – laying beyond the 'official' terms of the exposition or investigation. Such *associational* (and often *affective*) possibilities rely on an evaluative 'set' being already established in the viewer's mind and available for rapid evocation by 'trigger' words or images. That it would be perfectly possible for a reporter or directer plausibly to disclaim any intention to evoke such 'sets' of response in the viewer is a characteristic of this mode of discourse, giving it a strategic dimension. Such disclaiming is made possible because, whatever broader resonances of meaning are being produced, the choice of signifer is nearly always justifiable in terms of much more specific and narrow referential/representative functions (eg Hiroshima 1945 *is*, scientifically, a useful datum for arguments about radioactive dose-levels). In visual sequences, producers may even cite happenstance to support a claim of 'non- motivation' (dark storm clouds frequently *do* gather above the cooling towers of Sellafield).

As well as the range of quite generally applicable terms and images used by television (and by advertising) to generate affective responses in this way, there are sub-sets which have developed around specific topics, including that of nuclear power.

The use of particular place-names (eg Hiroshima, Three-Mile Island, Chernobyl), process descriptions (eg contamination, fail-safe, melt-down) and images (eg wire boundary fences, power stations next to mountain lakes, industrial installations at night) may serve not only to cue powerful local responses but also to frame the significance given to other other words and images, finally acting, perhaps, as an interpretative guide in reading the programme as a whole. Clearly, what we have referred to above as the 'sets' of response used by viewers are often resourced from a very wide inter- textual grid (in which, say, a sequence in the feature film, *The China Syndrome* or the BBC 'nuclear thriller' *Edge of Darkness*[13] might be more influential an immediate reference point than a recently seen documentary on energy sources).

Limiting discussion here to questions of visual imagery, and focussing on the projection of nuclear energy as *threatening*, we can note the prevalance of such

---

13 The China Syndrome *(Columbia, 1979) dramatised an operational flaw in a nuclear power plant with such narrative plausibility and acting power (Jane Fonda and Jack Lemmon) as to become a regular point of reference in later discussion of the Three-mile Island incident. Edge of Darkness, a series thriller broadcast by the BBC in 1986, was plotted around a secret reprocessing plant involving State conspiracy and multi-national finance. Its negative portrayal of nuclear industrialism, reinforced by 'sinister' visuals and an eerie musical score, could hardly have failed to make a contribution to popular understanding and feeling on the issue.*

material. Of the programmes we analysed, all but one of them (not suprisingly the CEGB promotional video) included shots which seemed to us to work associationally to produce strong negative feelings, as well as perhaps also working to constitute data within the logic of exposition. A very good example of such a shot would be one in *Uncertain Legacy* which we have described earlier. Here, after hovering above the surface of a lake adjacent to a nuclear power station, a lake which possesses a certain 'ghostly beauty' as a result of the steam rising from it, the camera slips below the surface to show, murkily, the bottom. The commentary meanwhile talks of 'a whole spectrum of nucleids...polluting the lower depths.' It is important to note here how what was picked up by many of our respondents as a very powerful depiction of 'unnaturalness' and 'hidden menace', is dependent on the speech soundtrack both for specific information and also for the figurative polarities (on top, visible natural beauty; underneath, invisible unnatural menace) around which its meanings are graphically clinched. Later shots in this programme, of work on a new reprocesssing plant and of piles of the waste *already* awaiting disposal, have enough self-evident referentiality to work with a minimum of narrational input, but here the use of music (slow tempo 'eerie electronic') reinforces the strength and direction of the response. If we take an example from *Heart of the Matter* – the very first shot of Sellafield, seen at a distance from a position on the edge of the Lake District fells – the negative effect here results from this shot's positioning immediately after a shot of a tranquil, wooded lakeside. This is further reinforced by the ironic turn of the commentary, which having talked of 'the natural life, the good life', shifts tone to note 'Well, that's how it *looks*' just as we are moved visually from lakeside idyll to a distant perception of something which is now imbued with *contrariness*. This articulation of threat by a contradistinction with previously established images of 'natural-ness' is, in fact, a key trope in generating extra-rational negative meaning and is the method used by *Uncertain Legacy* too, both in the example above and a further one offered below. It is also there in the organisation of *From Our Own Correspond-ent*, which is developed around a much more comprehensive and explicit 'threat' principle, but which employs a contradistinctive shift from highly 'composed' shots (e.g. long- take, steady camera, slow zooms) of trees, fields and cows to rawly 'immediate' shots of disaster and panic.

As one might expect, given its very different rhetorical brief, *Energy – the Nuclear Option* tries in its opening to give a musical and visual inflection of 'positive naturalness' to its depiction of the Sizewell coastline, an inflection which is an implicit *counter* to the subversive work of 'threat' rhetorics. One might, indeed, directly compare its portrayed beach, sunny and 'alive' with fishing activity and family walkers, with the beach near Sellafield in *Heart of the Matter*, the deserted character of which, given the commentary's point that this is the 'hottest day of the year', reads as *ominously* unpeopled. Documented local fact is here on the way to becoming general symbolic truth.

The opening of *Uncertain Legacy* articulates 'threat' but it does so not by any single 'high resonance' shot reinforced by commentary or music, but by a whole scenario of shots which depict a threatened community next to Hinkley Point power station. A peaceful ruralism (established by the depiction of cottage, church, village shop and village school) is being 'de-natured' by its proximity to the nuclear industry. This encroachment upon normality is signalled by shots of a clicking Geiger counter intercut with village scenes, by the sight of 'emergency plan' leaflets being put through letter-boxes and being carried in shopping baskets and also, most powerfully, by the presence in the school office of potassium iodate tablets for emergency use. The 'wrongness' of the situation is, we would argue, established at a level deeper than that at which the subsequent reportorial inquiry will be conducted. In that sense, such an implied scenario, coming right at the start of the programme, sets up a resonance of 'threat' which it would be difficult if not impossible for any subsequent 'findings' to cancel. There is, then, a powerful metonymic discourse of 'threat' around the nuclear industry, upon which television productions can draw. They may do this by the single, 'telling' shot or by a more elaborate articulation. In both cases, extra-visual signification may also be involved. Certainly, the powerful impact of Chernobyl upon public apprehensions of risk would seem to have extended the range and strength of negatively resonant images. As our respondent reports show, it would be most unwise to ignore their contribution to taken meanings.

Lessons from the past

Three key datum points in the history of nuclear power technology feature in these programmes: the 1957 Windscale fire in Britain; the 1979 Three-mile Island accident in the U.S.A., and the 1986 Chernobyl disaster in the Soviet Union. It is with the verbal and visual evocation of these events to some rhetorical purpose that we are here concerned. These single, potent, catastrophic incidents cannot be ignored either by protagonists or by antagonists of nuclear power, but they can be read in different ways, their relevance can be disputed, and they can be played 'up' or 'down'. Other datum points in popular memory can also be introduced to inflect the argument as required. *Energy – The Nuclear Option* reminds the viewers of the 1985 British miners' strike, with scenes of police-picket confrontation. The message here is that we must keep a nuclear capacity in Britain in case of interruptions to other fuel supplies. The 1974 Arab oil embargo is another reference point for this argument. *Uncertain Legacy* invites viewers to remember Hiroshima – the point of this (officially) is that medical research is still learning about radiation and risk from the effects upon the surviving victims.

Unofficially, of course, Hiroshima may provoke other reflections on technology and history.

In the context of a sequence on Downs' Syndrome cases in the vicinity of Sellafield, the Windscale fire is drawn into *Uncertain Legacy*'s textualisation through archive newsreel footage showing cows and people 'recovering' from its effects. The original narration of this newsreel is framed as *shockingly* upbeat – at best naive, at worst complicit with a policy of official secrecy. This event also finds its way into the presenter's catalogue of 'incidents' which constitute the negative side of the industry's safety record. He uses this catalogue to confront the BNFL chairman. But as far as the chairman is concerned:

> *There has been nobody killed in British Nuclear Fuels as a result of a radioactive incident in the last thirty years.*

The point of this phrasing is to indicate that the Windscale fire was a long time ago. There *have* been more recent deaths but radioactivity was not the cause. In *Heart of the Matter* the significance of Windscale is precisely the death-toll, not in itself a matter of dispute it seems. Bakewell is evoking Sellafield's poor safety record:

> *The 1957 fire at Windscale which burned out of control for at least 2 days certainly made the newsreels when milk from local firms had to be poured away. At the time the Government report was reassuring. Today's official estimate is that the fire was responsible for thirty-three deaths.*

Elsewhere, *Energy – The Nuclear Option* uses the fact that the fire happened in a BNFL military plant, not a CEGB civil one, to play down the significance of Windscale.

> *In over a quarter of a century of operation there is no evidence that any member of the public has been killed or injured by an accidental release of radioactivity at a CEGB nuclear power station.*

This is a version of the Windscale 'no deaths' thesis which builds in even more insurance against gainsaying by confining its scope to members of the public, thereby excluding the workers who were the Windscale victims.

The accident at Three-mile Island is remembered too. For *Uncertain Legacy*, the U.S. authorities come out very badly in retrospect, and in a way which further supports our comments on expert and ordinary perspectives:

> *Although the amounts of radioactivity released during the accident were said to be small, it's now clear that they weren't even properly measured. And while the official view is that no-one was harmed by Three-mile Island, people who live near the plant prefer to believe the evidence of their own eyes.*

By contrast *Energy – The Nuclear Option* accepts the official 'no harm' view, and goes on to address the question of whether a similar accident could happen at Sizewell B, also a PWR. It concludes, with support from the Layfield report, that the design is different and safer, thanks to Britain's more rigorous safety standards.

Chernobyl-in-Britain is a central concern in both *Energy – The Nuclear Option* and *From Our Own Correspondent*. The former argues explicitly that a Chernobyl-type accident is impossible in Britain. The latter assumes that a comparable event is perfectly possible, and addresses itself to the consequences rather than the causes. The relevance of Chernobyl in *From Our Own correspondent* has to do with the inadequacies of emergency planning in the event of a catastrophe. The British authorities, it suggests, have not recognised this relevance. The chaos would be even worse than at Chernobyl if Hartlepool's reactor got out of control, because of the size of the local population. Of course the reassurance of the other programme might be thought to render these particular anxieties superfluous. Dominant explanations for Chernobyl itself have two aspects: operator irresponsibility and reactor design. *Energy – The Nuclear Option* has a very strong line on the latter, which includes a degree of technical explanation:

> *The Russian reactor was known to be very unstable under some conditions. At low power it had what is known as a positive power coefficient. This means that if the power starts to rise from a low level it can suddenly surge to a high level in seconds. And this is what happened at Chernobyl during an unorthodox experiment when the reactor was being run at a very low power level.*

It handles the faults of the operators less directly, acknowledging briefly that the Russian operators were found irresponsible by the Soviet authorities, before moving on to reactor design. Later sections of the programme portray the rigorous training procedures for British operators and the fail-safe mechanisms that by implication would prohibit irresponsible operator actions. However, the human element is the weak link for many of our respondents. For instance, in the Conservative Party group the question is asked 'how do we know that some people couldn't do the same thing here?'

Finally, as we have noted earlier, when Lord Marshall, the CEGB chairman, is invited by Brian Walden to address the question of a possible British disaster, his response is to agree that a disaster is possible – just as an earthquake before the end of the interview is possible. The generality of this answer fails to address the fear of a Chernobyl-*scale* accident of a different *type*.

The wide range of variation and conflict in approach between these programmes is both substantive and discursive. Substantively, although there is some shared ground on the kind of 'knowledge' which constitutes the parameters of the nuclear debate, conflict about the status and meaning of that 'knowledge' is very apparent. Discursively, too, the approaches are very different, both at the level of general rhetorical strategies not unique to television as a medium, and in relation to the specific conventions of audiovisual discourse – the meaning of direct address from a news studio; the possibilities of intercut and contrastive images; the credibility values of particular speakers, etc. This variability has implications for the respondent study. It reinforces the expectation that respondents too will vary widely in their relations to the substance of the arguments. It also invites us to ask how far respondents vary in their relations to the discursive forms through which the arguments are mediated.

4 The Viewers

As we outlined in our introduction to this book, we wished to include as a primary element of our study an investigation into how viewers made sense of, and evaluated, the programmes we chose for analysis. 'Reception studies' have become an important part of media research in the last decade and before we indicate some of the details of our own research design, it might be worth commenting on a few of the general features of this area of inquiry.

To some extent, a growth of researcher interest in how viewers interpret what they see and hear can be seen as a re-connection with empirical modes of fieldwork research after a period in which the pursuit of general theory and of semiotic textual analyses held sway in British media studies. Researchers from sociology and social psychology, where an empirical concern with audiences has always been a principal research strand, would perhaps be inclined to view recent developments simply as a 'return'. However, this would be misleading. For what characterises the newer developments in reception study is an attention to the detail of significatory form (image and language) and to the 'creative' processes of interpretation of a kind not generally observable in the mainstream social science tradition. Without a doubt, the seminal text for this new strand of work is David Morley's *The 'Nationwide' Audience* !14 published in 1980 Modest enough in scope, and working with a sometimes vulnerably mechanistic idea of interpretation as 'decoding', this study nevertheless explored in new and provocative ways the processes by which text-reader interaction produces socially differentiated meaning and it has rightly been one of the most cited and discussed works in international media research over the last decade.

Our reception study is conceived within the broad framework of the Morley venture, though with considerable differences in some of the guiding ideas and analytic methods. Nevertheless, in the context of 1990 there are two good reasons for us to note a continuity with his 1980 investigations. First of all, we are mostly concerned, as he was, with reading practices which are brought to bear on

---

14 *David Morley* The 'Nationwide' Audience: structure and decoding, *London, British Film Institute 1980.*

non-fiction television, where the interplay between 'story' and 'fact', imagination and knowledge, textuality and reference, is likely to be different from that of, say, popular series drama. This difference, and its implications for positions and practices of 'reading', does not seem to us to be sufficiently recognised in a number of recent audience studies which, though looking primarily at Soap Opera, have nevertheless appeared to want to construct a general theory of reception. Secondly, following Morley's 1986 study, *Family Television*,[15] there has been a move in research towards investigating the domestic conditions of television use: routines, programme preferences and the range of activities co-extensive with viewing. As part of a broader anthropology of domestic culture as well as of an inquiry into determinants of the television process, this is wholly to be welcomed. In our view, however, its recognition of contextual difference and interactive variety should not displace the usefulness of conducting studies which attempt to plot the process of meaning production by looking at the relationship between specific programmes and viewer understanding and response. These studies, usually requiring the playback of taped material, have a quasi-experimental character to them which may seem false to the 'real'. But of course, nearly all socially investigative methods require an intervention into the very processes they wish to document – the creation of heightened awareness in the respondent, the requirement for people in some way or other to 'give an account of themselves', the setting up of 'artificial' situations. If researchers feel that, nevertheless, something of what is generated in their inquiries bears significantly on habits, meanings and processes going on independently of their interventionary sampling, then all they can do is be self-aware, cautious and honest in their practices. In drafting and applying our research design and in writing up our accounts we have tried, at least, to be all three.

Research design

We envisaged the sample audience for these programmes in terms that emphasised the most *relevant* aspects of their social identities – relevant, that is, for projecting their potential engagement with the topic of the programmes.

With this in mind, our sampling was oriented, in the first instance, to what may broadly be termed 'interest groups'. We anticipated that the main political parties would have reason to be interested in this topic (even though nuclear energy is not a simple partisan issue). We accordingly obtained the participation of respondent groups from the local Labour, Conservative and SLD parties. The net was extended to groups from the local Rotary club, one from the Labour and Trade Union Resource Centre of unemployed people, a women's discussion group, a group of comprehensive school pupils, a group of medical students,

---

15 *David Morley* Family Television: cultural power and domestic leisure, *London, Comedia 1986.*

some Friends of the Earth members and a set of workers at the Heysham nuclear power plant. In addition to these groups, which we treated as 'pre-constituted' groups for the purposes of the research since the members were already acquainted with one another, we recruited individuals on Merseyside into four mixed, 'researcher-constituted' groups. These were mainly shop floor workers in local industries such as Fords and Littlewoods. We also conducted four sessions with individuals during a pilot study exercise prior to Phase One and based upon the same programmes. We have made very little use of these, except for an occasional quotation in the final section of this chapter.

For the second phase study there were three participating groups: one involving the local Womens' Institute and two involving first year students at Liverpool University – one of Arts students and one of Science students.

The research sessions themselves were quasi-experimental in that, first of all, the circumstances of the viewings were non-naturalistic. Respondent groups generally came to the department, or we met them in their headquarters. Occasionally, sessions took place in the home of a respondent, but a home de-naturalised by the presence of the group as a whole, and of the researchers. Secondly, Phase One of the study was designed to elicit comparisons between the three programmes screened. This was done in full recognition that it would provoke higher levels of attention to programme *form* than if each programme had been screened singly.

Groups were primed to expect material on 'a topic of current interest', not specifically nuclear energy. Sessions, which were audiotaped, began by eliciting general views on the topic, then proceeded with the programme screenings (three programmes in Phase One of our study, one in Phase Two). This was followed each time by periods of semi- structured discussion around a common, basic agenda which we had prepared and then kept standard for each group, totalling about 50 minutes. We tried to elicit reactions on aspects of interest to us whilst at the same time allowing the groups to develop themes according to their own agendas. The Phase One programmes were screened in the order in which we discuss them above: *Uncertain Legacy*; *Energy – the Nuclear Option*; *From Our Own correspondent*. The relative advantages of group-based and individual-based respondent sessions has been a subject of much discussion in the literature. For the present study, the advantage of the group-based approach was the opportunity it offered for participants to negotiate with one another their often conflicting responses to the programmes screened. This keeps in focus the potential for divergence as well as convergence within sets of people who were participating as representatives of organisations. We are of course sensitive to the possibility that in some cases this may work to to *produce* more consensus than might otherwise be the case.

The investigation of meaning in reception studies needs to differentiate analytically between 'understanding' and 'response', however interfused these may be in practice. For it is of course entirely possible for viewers to agree as to how to understand an item but to disagree in their responses to it. Less obviously, it is also possible for viewers to appear to share a response yet (perhaps unknown to each other) to hold to different basic understandings of what they have seen and heard.[16] In practice, there is often a kind of 'to and fro' incrementalism at work by which meanings which have been processed into responses by viewers then 'act back' to constitute the reading frame for the reception of subsequent 'primary' understandings. In our study, rather than *separate* analysis off into two phases, we have tried to be alert to the incremental and meaning/value shifts.

We have characterised our approach as 'ethnodiscursive'. This indicates, on the one hand, the ethnographic basis of our sampling, and on the other, the close attention we have paid to the language used by the respondents in articulating and negotiating their responses to the programmes. Although we have not made use of any tightly categoric scheme of analysis we have found the notion of 'frame' a helpful one with which to approach the data. Respondents appropriate the programmes, or aspects of them, from within particular frameworks of understanding, which supply them with criteria of evaluation both for programme forms and contents. Central among these is what we have termed the 'civic' frame, concerned with propriety in addressing a national audience on a controversial topic. Within that frame, the major but not exclusive criterion of evaluation is that of 'balance'. Other frameworks that seem to us to be variously operative across the groups include a more directly *political* frame (subsuming an *environmentalist* orientation), a *personal* frame, and an *evidential* one, having a primary concern with the status of evidence and argument. Our way of using these 'frames' as broadly classificatory will be apparent in the accounts which follow.

Conservative Party Group

(This group consisted of two men and two women)

1. Uncertain Legacy

The group's initial response to this programme is largely a critical one and it is made within a version of what we have discussed above as the *civic* framing, a framing both of television programmes as public communication and of the topic itself as a public issue. Here are two opening responses from members of the group:

---

16 *For a discussion of this and other theoretical issues on reception research see John Corner 'Cultural Power and the "Reception" Problematic in Recent Media Research' in James Curran and Michael Gurevitch (eds)*Mass Communication and Society (Second edition) London, Edward Arnold *(forthcoming).*

A. I thought it was rather unbalanced because it was basically all anti-nuclear. I would have liked to have seen some very experienced scientists also giving their side. Because the CEGB man was only saying what he had been told to say. He didn't have any deep knowledge of it. So I felt it was too unbalanced.

B. I thought it was very inconclusive, it didn't come down really, in fact, no I'll rephrase that, it seemed to be coming down more heavily against the use of nuclear power from the possibilities of harm to human beings. I would very much like to have seen a debate at the end or somewhere in the programme for the pros and cons – some people who are involved and very knowledgeable debating with some people of anti-nuclear energy [views].

A number of themes emerge here, connecting this group's perspective on television's impartiality requirements to its views on scientific authority (and its suspicions that the programme has here been neglectful). At a general level, this connection can be seen to be one in which the group's *civic* frames of reference link up with its framings of the *evidential*.

Resistance to the programme appears to be partly *procedural*, a belief that a formal obligation to show 'the other side' has not been honoured, and partly *substantive*, in that it is believed the presence of more authoritative, expert assessment would have got closer to the truth of the matter than the programme managed with its chosen speakers. Speaker B's comments seem to show a tension between a desire for truthfulness (as against the 'inconclusive') and a desire for a balancing of 'pros and cons'. Perhaps it is precisely the degree of 'conclusiveness' in what the speaker feels to be an *erroneous* direction that underlies this contradictoriness of judgement.

That what *is* shown and said exerts a degree of persuasive force is directly testified to by one respondent:

A. I mean you must take note of the evidence presented to you and that seems to be, I won't say evidence you can't dispute because of course Lord Marshall and the managing director of Sellafield proved the opposite case I suppose. The evidence was rather more one side than the other and I suppose that in itself influences you.

A number of group members speculate, without reaching a clear decision, on the extent to which this 'one-sidedness' was either the product of the unavailability of certain types of speaker or of a prior motivation to present a negative case. There is evidence that this troubled concern with what is missing is partly the product of the group judging as unsatisfactory the contribution made to the programme by the most senior proponent of Nuclear Energy to appear, Lord Marshall. Despite the comment of the last quoted respondent that, against the main persuasive drift of the programme, Marshall 'proved the opposite case, I suppose' (the uncertainty here is significant) response to his interview is unanimously negative:

B. I was rather sorry that Lord Marshall in that film appeared to be treating it rather lightly. I didn't feel that was fitting to the subject...just from his manner you knew he was brushing off things.

C. He was flippant.

B. I thought that.

C. He should have tried much harder to disprove some of the statements.

D. I thought that when he said you can put it in my garden [a waste site] he was saying that because he knew there was no likelihood.

'Imbalance' is also perceived as a feature of the programme's images. One speaker notes an unfair use of archive footage of the Atom bomb tests:

A. Well, that's another aspect of it being one-sided. We had brought home to us all the horror of the A-bomb, that was relating in our minds from that to nuclear energy.

But this detection of manipulative, rhetorical (and here, 'emotive') intent does not prevent other images in the programme securing an effect. For instance, following the comment above, another speaker, continuing the theme of the programme's visual exposition, refers to the Trawsfynnedd lake sequence (see discussion in chapters 3 and 4) and the disturbing sense of pollution which the images carried. Given our earlier discussion of this sequence, it is of interest that this reference, though brief and rather fragmented, appears to understand the problem as being one of the lake's official use as a dumping ground for nuclear waste:

C. They were talking about the lake weren't they? Trawsfynnedd. And that presumably was put at the bottom of the lake in some of these... I understood they were lead containers. The lake is supposed to be affected already.

2. Energy – The Nuclear Option

The particular 'civic' framing within whose terms *Uncertain Legacy* is registered as unbalanced is again brought to bear in the discussion of this programme, producing what might seem to be a suprising degree of critical comment on its 'opposite but equal' bias given the previously expressed desire of the group to see a 'fair hearing' accorded to the pro-nuclear position. The programme's status as a corporate promotional video does not, for this group, win for it the license to be 'one-sided' however. Indeed its emphatic advocacy of nuclear energy eventually produces a more strongly-phrased critical response from most group members than did the first programme screened.

C. It was the other side of the story wasn't it ? It was supply and demand and safety this time.

B. There used to be a series on Sunday morning with Brian Walden. I feel that was just as much prejudiced to the other side. They referred to other methods of energy, the windmills and they said these would be an eyesore and make noises but they can't be much more of an eyesore than the actual places ... Frankly, they'd made up their minds saying it was nuclear energy they were interested in.

D. They made it out that it was almost inevitable to my way of thinking that we were going to have it and it wasn't quite as bad as people thought. Certainly it was more on the other side.

The subsequent discussion contains some quite sharply contrasting responses: one member notes, for instance, that 'I just felt we were being brainwashed quite frankly', while another adopts a more deferent (if still uneasy) attitude, 'And so I mean we as lay people have got to sometimes accept what the experts say, I mean you can't query them.'

The 'civic' critique applied to *Uncertain Legacy* was in response to a structured 'bias' whose degree of motivation was unclear, that applied to *Energy – the Nuclear Option* becomes one in response to elements of the propagandistic. The changed terms of negotiation and (often) of rejection are shown in the discussion of the role of Brian Walden as the presenter. One member regarded the choice of Walden as being that of 'an experienced man to brainwash you' and whilst there was recognition of his skill and professionalism, the connection of these qualities with authority or indeed with any personal authenticity was questioned. Another speaker, commenting on the presentation, found it significant to note of Walden that 'he was being paid' (with clear implications for any civic framing of the integrity of his comments) whilst another observed:

B. He might be just as good telling you how terrible things were.

The same speaker developed a 'boomarang' account of the effect of the programmes emphasis on safety, with particular reference to two points in the exposition. First of all, in relation to the way in which the programme referenced Chernobyl:

B. And they kept on referring.. that the accident that happened in Chernobyl could not happen here. Now the accident in Chernobyl was absolutely due to negligence on the part of the operators who decided they were going to try out some experiment. So how do we know that some people couldn't do the same thing here ?

Secondly, in relation to the filmed sequence on safety mechanisms and procedures which occurs towards the end of the programme:

B. It still comes over as very tainted you know. They were so reassuring that they'd done everything possible.. it wouldn't be necessary if it wasn't such a dangerous way of producing energy.

Clearly, we can extend the notion of viewer framing to observe that what happens with this viewer's reading (and it occurs elsewhere in other groups) is that a pre-established 'risk' framing is triggered by those very items from which the programme seeks to promote a generalized interpretation of 'safety'.

More generally within the group, Lord Marshall's performance is judged critically despite the impossibility here of seeing this partly as a function of hostile context. In fact, this group is among those in which at least one member regards his answer to Walden's 'bomb' question (see our discussion in Chapter 4) not only as unsatisfactory but as revealing, in the blatancy of its perceived 'gaffe', of a more general inadequacy of account:

> B. Well, I thought he said, Lord Marshall said 'Well, it doesn't explode like a bomb you know' and then in the next breath he said 'the top blew off of Chernobyl'.

3. From Our Own Correspondent

This *Northern Newsreel* item immediately provoked a strong negative response among the group and it was the *political* motivations which they detected at work in the piece which were most prominent in initial reactions. To that degree, we can see their response here as shifting from matters of civics and relations of knowledge to a more openly political engagement.

> B. I would say it was a very biassed politically motivated group. And I would render (sic) to suggest that it was something to do with the trade unions.

> D. It was very interesting to hear the character blaming the government and the CEGB.

Unlike *Uncertain Legacy*, which is treated as unbalanced, and *Energy – The Nuclear Option*, which is seen as, in part, ineffectively propagandistic, the *Northern Newsreel* treatment is seen right from the start as an attempted *political* hi-jacking of the debate, an item with 'an ulterior motive'. The details of its production, distribution and use immediately become the subject of inquiry and discussion among group members. Two other factors interconnect with this political framing of the response. First of all, as in several other groups, the limited production qualities of the tape are commented on in a way which, without being explicitly argued, lends support to the dismissal of its informing ideas. Secondly, its strategy as a fiction causes both a degree of confusion about what actually *did* happen at Hartlepool and considerable suspicion about what are seen to be its deceptive intentions:

> B. A lot of it was fiction and unfortunately I believe that there are some people who would see that film and would really and truly believe that it had happened. I would be far more interested to know the organisation behind it and the use to which it is being put.

Other group members talk of 'garbage for the masses', 'fifth columnists' and 'propaganda', whilst one observes that 'I know this is a democratic country but sometimes democracy goes too far here'.

The question of production quality and manipulative design are brought together in apparently rhetorical speculation as to 'who would be taken in by the film', a speculation which then turns back on its own dismissiveness with the comment that 'a lot of people might be'.

That the approach of the piece is to appeal to the emotions is registered by members of the group as a further aspect of its illegitimacy:

> B. And the child having leukaemia and having to leave the dog, they're all very small points but they would register...It's appealing to your emotions, which are you know, emotions aren't sometimes the basis that one should form a judgement on are they? And a certain amount of hysteria is developed in that film and again we shouldn't be making absolute judgements from a hysterical..and it was very confusing and I think most people would find it very confusing to try to sort out.

Given the terms of our earlier discussion we can see this as a rejection of the appropriateness of the 'personal' framing for the handling of this topic, either by broadcasters or by viewers.

There is some discussion about the information concerning contingency zones with which the film ends but this is marginalized both by the level of antipathy felt towards the project as a whole and by a continuing confusion over the fact/fiction borderlines.

Summary

What group members regard as the under-representation of qualified scientific testimony becomes their major point of comment within a basic civic framing and is linked, as we have shown, to their expressed belief that such testimony would be likely to provide positive and trustworthy assessments of nuclear energy of the kind they are not able to find in any of the material screened. For this group, advocacy from within the industry itself and its hired public relations specialists is no substitute for such reassurance and the promotional strategies of *Energy – The Nuclear Option* are largely rejected, even though many of the substantive themes and assumptions of this programme coincide with their own, certainly much more so than the investigative scepticism of *Uncertain Legacy* or the dramatized alarmism of the *Northern Newsreel* item. No members of this group express a full confidence in the present levels of safety or in the honesty and integrity of those charged with public responsibilities in the industry. Without question, the most regularly cited substantive factor is that of 'waste', the absence of comment on which is thought to be an important limitation of *Energy – The Nuclear Option*. At one point suspicion is generalized, with group assent, into what might be regarded as a remarkably cynical assessment of the situation for a group so committed to established constitutional processes.

C. You don't know where you are. There's not much honest information given.

Labour Party Group

(This group consisted of two women and three men)

1. Uncertain Legacy

The initial response of group members is concerned with an assessment of how the programme's account squares with their own knowledge and views. Once again, however, as we found elsewhere, a civic sense of the need both for a 'fair' representation of contending factors and for propriety of treatment is installed as the primary perspective. As we also note in our account of other groups, the tension between this perspective and a more 'partial' one, reflecting members own dispositions and attitudes, forms a key feature of subsequent debate, if not always explicitly so. For speaker A the programme is inadequate because it has too limited an agenda and is guilty of omitting important aspects of the issue:

> *A. Well it didn't tell me anything I didn't know, I think it missed out a few things. It was just centred on whether people were going to die or not and there's more issues than that. There's this issue of people needing energy. I mean, I'm not a .. I don't believe in nuclear energy but I can see that there is a problem with a lot of people not having it. I don't think it went into that. It didn't talk about acid rain which is also a problem.*

The play-off in this comment, between a statement of current position and the recognition of factors which problematize that position (here, the huge scale of energy requirements, especially in developing countries, and the environmental hazard posed by fossil fuel sources) indicate the operation of 'civic' criteria with a useful explicitness. Against these criteria, the programme is found wanting. Other speakers, whilst using the same broad principles of assessment, disagree with this view by pointing to the legitimacy of the programme being highly selective in the interests of retaining a clear focus:

> *B. I thought the opposite in one sense. I accept what [A] said but I thought it was actually very thorough in the sense that it didn't quite, I don't know whether objectively is the right word, but quite calmly tried to examine what evidence there was from simply that point of view of the potential risks to health if you like, to human health. More in terms of people living around state power stations, that seemed to be the main emphasis. It didn't say anything about the much more global dangers, if something went wrong which it obviously has done in one or two cases. It didn't say anything about the effects on the people who actually work there. But you know, given its very particular purpose I thought it handled it well.*

This comment sparks off discussion on what might constitute a good programme on a topic like this, revealing some interesting differences in perceptions of rhetorical strategy and efficiency:

A. You don't know what happened, what went on behind the scenes.

C. I was of the opinion strangely that that programme, it was very bad because it defeated its own ends. It was too much anti- nuclear. Now you see what happens – it's talking to the converted. Now people who are pro-nuclear watching that, 'Oh this is a load of rubbish,' they'd say, 'Its nonsense, I don't want that, switch it off.' A more subtle mind, a more insidious way, perhaps. Like, 'I'm objective now, I'm not for or against, here are the facts.' I don't think programmes like that do anything, whether it's anti-bomb or anti-anything, that are so obviously weighted, to do our case any good.

D. I think the subject's so horrendous and the facts so frightening that we should see them as they are. I don't see....

C. Yes but you must get a manner of presenting so that the people who are indifferent to it would watch it.

B. I don't agree with you.. I don't think it was heavily biassed. Certainly not in relation to the degree of bias both in quantity and quality that goes the other way.

Disagreement here concerns not only the matter of how best to persuade those viewers who will come to the programme with pro-nuclear attitudes but also, in a secondary vein, the matter of how far it is facts rather than opinions which the programme deals in. Both C and B shift away from the civic frame in order to make the case for countervailing persuasive tactics. However, C clearly feels that the obviousness of the programme's anti-nuclear stance is a block to effective persuasion (a more 'insidious', overt approach having stronger potential). Incidentally, C's comments show a feature of respondent talk which importantly connects with ideas about *social difference* in TV interpretation. This is the 'displaced' reading – whereby a programme is evaluated in terms of the reading which people other than the respondent, bringing to bear different predispositions and understandings, will make.[17]

As might be expected from a group having both an anti-nuclear inclination and a political distrust of conventional styles of official, bureacratic reassurance, there is a certain relish taken in what is perceived as the negative performance of Lord Marshall. Interestingly,the poorness of this performance is seen as partly authentic and partly a function of the programme's depictive tactics. Clearly, they may be differences here in individual respondent perceptions:

B. I thought what came out most strongly is what idiots the most senior people emerged as, particularly Marshall...The chairman of the BNFL smugly smiling as he lied his way through the nonsense that he was speaking. I mean that was disgraceful.

17 *We made use of this concept in previous work, discussing the responses of selected Liverpool viewers to a programme about unemployment on Merseyside. See Kay Richardson and John Corner 'Reading reception: mediation and transparency in viewers' accounts of a TV programme'.* Media, Culture and Society *v 8, (1986) 485-508.*

and

C. I think he (Taylor) was marvellous getting that chairman bloke to look a complete and utter idiot.

Insofar as the programme's ending is found inconclusive, this group attribute inconclusiveness to the nature of the topic itself and do not therefore find the programme at fault. Furthermore, lack of conclusive proof does not necessarily strengthen the pro-nuclear case:

D. They kept saying, 'Nothing can be proved by all these children having cancers, nothing can be proved.' But they didn't say it can be disproved either.

In the absence of proof, questions of probability become central to the sway of debate:

E. ...he did say it was inconclusive, but just the coincidence really to me, all they did say it seems to be more than a coincidence, they hinted it was more than a coincidence."

2. Energy – The Nuclear Option

Consistent with his previous remarks, speaker A once more employs a strong civic frame and makes an initial assessment which contrasts with the one he made of *Uncertain Legacy*:

A. I enjoyed that one. I thought it was more informative and I think it gave a more balanced view...It did let people make up their minds.

The rest of the group do not share this interpretation and voice strong criticisms of bias, opening up a gap between A's reading and everyone else's which was to be significant in the pattern of the subsequent discussion:

E. No, I don't think so, he kept saying something about the benefits and the risks and I thought for the first sort of ten minutes or what ever, fifteen minutes, 'well right we're getting the benefits', it was all the benefits and at the end of the programme we still hadn't heard the risks. They didn't tell us any of the risks. They just said, 'oh yes and there's a little bit of a risk in Russia.'

As this negative evaluation continues, the persuasive tactics of the text are recognised and condemned :

B. I thought that what he was doing all the time was quite correctly raising the questions but then he proceeded to answer them in his own way, and gave the answers he thought we ought to be having...he shouldn't have answered them.

After we disclosed to the group that this was a promotional video rather than a broadcast programme, the discussion shifted to an assessment of the item as a calculated piece of propaganda. Having been seen as responding positively to its apparent impartiality, A now regards the piece as 'well done' because it has worked on him. Others in the group also appreciate the quality of its imitation of broadcast formats, finding it to be 'extremely clever' (C) in this respect. Once assured of the programme's partisan origins, the group become freer to articulate a more directly political response, now remembering the use of protestors and miners as negative images in the video. Even when it is regarded as an impressive, professional exercise in persuasion, certain limitations are noted:

> B. *The basic thing of any programme is 'show don't tell', Walden was telling all the time. And you either, you can take a certain amount of telling but then you cut off anyway.*

Moreover one of the central tenets of the programme, those key points upon which the attempt at authoritative, reassurance depends, is not only rejected but found risible:

> C. *'It can't happen in our country'(in a voice parodying programme).*

> E. *That was it.*

> B. *Yes that's right, the laws of physics don't allow it to happen in our country .... the laws of physics are different in Russia you see. (satirically delivered, followed by laughter)*

3. From Our Own Correspondent

The first reactions were a mixture of enjoyment in the drama and admissions of confusion as to the precise status of is what is seen and heard:

> A. *Oh I enjoyed it, I thought it was good.*

> C. *Yes I enjoyed it.*

> E. *I think I'm a bit puzzled by it.*

> C. *It was really drama.*

> E. *It wasn't particularly good drama.*

> D. *I didn't know whether it was real or not.*

> A. *You know at the end though.*

> D. *Oh yes it suddenly clicked.*

> B. *What it raises for me is the whole question about what is actually true and what isn't.*

D and E do not see the 'play' as at all effective, it is too 'messy' for them. Other members of the group are wary of the dangers of letting the fact of low-budget production affect a sympathetic overall response to the item's perspectives and ideas. B notes, by way of response to charges of poor technical quality:

B. But doesn't that show you what you expect from television because the technical standards are so high that if you see something that creaks a bit at the edges then that actually reduces its credibility, which is an appalling thing actually if that's what we're doing.

Civic framings, with their language of balance and bias, do not here provide critical leverage, because the perceived anti-nuclear bias of the item is such that it 'didn't try to be anything else' and is therefore not accountable in the same way as the previous two progammes. However, the discussion ends with a criticism of the extent to which *From Our Own Correspondent* is guilty of 'feeding on people's emotional fears'. Such a judgement is in a certain amount of tension with the fact that no one seemed to have found this aspect of it particularly effective and group members were more frightened by the approach of *Uncertain Legacy*. Once again, it is a 'displaced' reading, one that might be made by other viewers, which appears to underlie this judgement, although it is of course perfectly possible to criticise intention whilst noting ineffectiveness of execution.

Summary

This group, like others we worked with, operates within a fundamentally civic perception of how the issue should be dealt with in public debate and (therefore) of how it should be presented on television. An exception is made for *From Our Own Correspondent*, which is licensed in its partisan account both by virtue of its status an imaginative work (as 'drama') and its self-admittance of polemical intent (though in normal viewing circumstances, this would at least as much be a function of its distribution context – a subscription video service – as of textual markers). The civic framing is in potential conflict with a partisan, political framing, which may understandably hold to certain disputed points as 'facts of the matter' and cannot therefore see everything as being really 'open to debate', however desirable this might be as a procedural convention. Clearly, members of the group differ in their weighting of civic against partisan perspectives and the three items screened play into this difference in such a way as to cause further differentiation both in respect of criteria of propriety and criteria of effectiveness. One of the characteristics of the discussion, which can at least partly be seen in the above quotations, is the extent to which Speaker A's evaluations tend to differ from those of other group members. This can be attributed, among other things, to the degree to which A feels the case for nuclear power *is* worthy of being seriously entertained. Another feature of the group's discussion, not suprising in active members of a political party, is the close attention given to the 'tactics' by which a public issue is debated and a consequent reluctance to assume the deference towards authority which certain kinds of pronouncements in the programmes appear to presume.

Rotary Group

(This group consisted of five men)

1. Uncertain Legacy

This group moves directly into an assessment of the programme as technically very good, and as partisan against nuclear energy. Technical merit is separated from merit in the substance of argument. Initially it is the statistical basis of the presenter's argument which is challenged:

> A. *I think about the statistics they used, they said themselves part way through they're always suspect, that you can manipulate statistics to make almost any case you choose, therefore that didn't make a case for me, it made me suspicious of the case and I think I would have liked to have heard someone else produce counter statistics.*

The benefit of the doubt will not readily be given by this group to the 'victims' – they want more, or more reliable, evidence (for they do not register an ultimate inconclusiveness sufficient to problematise the very possibility of resolution). Later, it is the industry's statistical arguments which are disparaged as 'even barmier' than the programme's own. Many members of the group draw on their own expert knowledge in assessing the programmes:

> B. *My knowledge of the American legal system would lead me to believe that the evidence produced around that Three-mile Island incident was actually counter productive and makes me less likely to believe the general thesis....And certainly that case of the Downs' Syndrome child, the majority of Downs' children are actually born to young women.*

Another line of criticism involves foregrounding what the programme did *not* deal with, implying that to have done so would have undermined its negative thrust.

> B. *You can find clusters elsewhere not apparently associated. It may not lessen the fact that it is a little bit worrying that anyone near there should have been affected if they have been.*

The logic of comparative risk is invoked at one point (by the speaker who is the most sympathetic to the industry):

> C. *What a marvellous case you could make for the abolition of motor transport, think of how many people's lives we could save if only we abolished that.*

They also react unfavourably to imagery perceived as manipulatory:

> B. *A bit trite, sort of murmured threat and silk-like beauty with little cottages...the symbolism was a bit too obvious...dominated by the visual material apropos the music apropos what was being said, the scenes and the mood setting was I think I thought I was being dragged through the nose (sic) a little.*

61

Yet they do not, in challenging the programme, find the partisan standpoint it adopts to be an illegitimate one, nor do they entirely reject the propositions that underlie its provocations to anxiety:

> A. It's going through a couple of aspects, our lack of understanding of the effects of low levels of radiation, and perhaps it's worse than we think. And I think the other one which is still skating round a little bit is, what do you do with it all when you've finished with it, what do you do with a power station? .....What do you do with a blooming great power station, tens of thousands of tons of steel and concrete? So I'd like somebody to tell me in a little bit more detail what's .... It's those practical aspects which concern me more, I think, whether you can make a better case ....

2. Energy – The Nuclear Option

This is immediately perceived as overtly pro-nuclear power although how soon they realise it is an industry film is unclear. Their own, qualified, pro-nuclear views do not lead to a sympathetic hearing for the programme as a whole. They are highly critical of both Walden and Marshall:

> A. Brian Walden came over as either a Cleaneasy man who calls at the door or somebody lecturing at nursery school.

> B. Well for someone who has totally changed his political viewpoint from Labour to far right Thatcherism, I mean, would you actually buy a Cleaneasy off him never mind the British Nuclear industry?

> D. I thought that was marvellous that was, we've got the best nuclear power programme in the world and around every station the sun shines all the time. (parody of Marshall)

> B. And I don't believe these statistics and in any case there's probably just as many around the Coal Board. (continued parody)

Walden also lacks conviction for them as a 'paid' voice in this production. As for other groups, the tone is found patronising, and the 'boomerang' effect again comes into play for one respondent who feels less confident about the industry having seen this programme. Speaker C believes in the industry's technical safety standards, not on the basis of this programme but from direct personal experience. Yet this belief is not on its own enough to constitute for him a defence against such challenges as the above, with which he seems to concur although he does not initiate them. His allegiance to the industry shows up, rather, in his repetitions of arguments initiated by the pro-industry spokesmen in the programme, like Marshall's argument that, where risk is concerned, there can be no absolute guarantees that an accident is not possible. This may reflect a 'consensus effect' within the group: in such critical company, only with great difficulty could he take a strongly contrary position. Their efforts as a group to give credit where due, so to speak, are in evidence when another speaker contrasts the programme with *Uncertain Legacy*, favouring it for its greater factual content:

> A. *The second programme did explain about the technical aspects of nuclear power stations, it did explain about different types and it did relate the problem of Chernobyl to the ones in this country...whereas the first programme was all emotive, it never got involved in simple technical explanation.*

3. From Our Own Correspondent

Recognition of emotional appeal, confusion at the shifts of time and place and of fact and fiction, and a negative response to poor technical quality, all feature in the group's response to this item. Confusion is registered in initial comments, then amplified:

> D. *We know that in great parts of that they were playacting...so how can you tell which is the facts from which is the playacting?*

> A. *As a communication exercise that film left me completely unmoved because I didn't know whether they were condemning the CEGB, whether it was condemning the government...I didn't know what they were trying to get at...I think this was the overdramatic way they presented it, I think it was having it presented as being interviewed by a Russian, I thought 'well this is play- acting, are any of the facts that are reported are they based on the truth or are they,..?'*

The fictional treatment is here registered as destroying any possibility of evaluation in substantive terms. Another speaker then posits different grounds of evaluation:

> C. *I don't think they're trying to present anything factual, its an emotional appeal, to try and put yourself in the situation. They did also mention that a fairly major accident had happened at Hartlepool.*

They reject the item, though not as an illegitimate exercise in persuasion. Speaker B defends the 'directness' of the emotional appeal for the purpose of breaking through established ideas. But that is to defend intention, not execution or effect:

> B. *Having people with very fixed ideas, I think the way to overcome and break through that might be to sort of try an emotional approach which is very direct like this, it's going to irritate some people, amuse others, it might make some people change, I don't know.*

The rejection derives rather from the item's incompatibility with their evidential concerns, and from their perception of its technical (and its aesthetic) quality as weak. For all the group the technical quality is a problem and their reluctance to accept the fiction is couched in generational terms – younger people would appreciate it more. This is seen as a factor for concern by some group members who believe that it is younger people who are the most impressionable, implying that to be impressed by this type of film is not a good thing.

Summary

Concern with evidence and argument dominates the first two accounts, so when the group come to *From Our Own Correspondent* they have initial difficulties in finding an appropriate standpoint from which to evaluate it. Their frequent recourse to knowledge which they possess as professionals in relevant areas such as medicine is very striking, and goes along with the identification of 'missing' information which is neither explicit in the programmes nor available to them independently of it, but which is nevertheless considered necessary if an informed judgment is to be made. Whilst each programme is perceived as legitimate on its own terms, nothwithstanding its bias, civic concerns are evident in the efforts made by this group to give credit for quality of presentation and argument even if at odds with their own sympathies. Such concerns tend to shift some of the responsibility for 'fairness' from the programmes to themselves as viewers. They require themselves to be open to both sides of the argument.

Unemployed group

(This group consisted of three men and three women)

1. Uncertain Legacy

Although this group begins by characterising the programme as biased, they are also swift to identify specific, unsatisfactory elements of the case made out by the nuclear industry's representatives within the programme. They suggest that there are too few interviewees on the pro-nuclear side: yet the ones who did contribute produced only 'stupid' analogies of anonymous origin.

> C. *I think it was a little unfair to be honest with you because pro-nuclear people were just like business-men or whatever. By and large. There was an inspector but the anti-nuclear people were by and large scientific, so the arguments were different so it was a little unfair on the chairman of BNFL...I would have preferred to have seen scientists from BNFL being interviewed as well.*

> D. *And workers too. They didn't ask any workers about how they felt about actually being on site. Their opinion wasn't taken into account at all.*

> B. *They (industry representatives) all referred to unknown people to support their argument because they were making stupid analogies you know, like it's saying, smoking one ciggy in your lifetime, and then they were just saying well we get the best advice possible, the best scientists, but they still remained anonymous*

There is a tension within the group between C and the others, with C being more critical:

> *C. The thing that didn't convince me, though, was he didn't compare it with things in the coal industry, deaths in the oil industry or whatever....*

> *B. I think the argument he used was the best one you could use, that you don't invent something that you've got no way of controlling, no contingency plan and absolutely no idea of how you're going to deal with the problem.*

C here is evidently assessing the programme in terms of its 'fairness' as a forum for discussion whilst B assesses it primarily in terms of it being an argument about the truth, the adequacy of which can be judged against the speaker's pre-established sense of just where this lies.

Towards the end of the discussion, C and B appear almost to 'change places' in respect of the value they put upon impartiality:

> *C. I don't know where that bloke's (the presenter's) coming from. He seemed to be anti but he didn't actually say at the beginning. I think it would have been better if he'd stated that he was going to make a critical analysis of it. Maybe it would have been better if someone from Greenpeace had been on – I mean you would know what they were actually about and...you're aware of what sort of cases they're arguing.*

> *B. I don't agree with that because what you're looking for in a programme is a kind, as far as possible, I think is an impartiality from the person..*

> *C. I don't think you can be impartial*

> *B. No you can't but as largely as possible, even if he's got an anti-nuclear energy view really, what he wants is all his arguments tested in front of the the viewers so that you're going to share his views but not from a totally biassed start, from a more impartial start.*

What in fact seems to happen is that B and C's original positions get developed out and modified in the course of reacting to the opposing view. C's stress on a civic integrity is still maintained in his argument that the programme would have done better to declare its critical view from the outset or else have it represented by a Greenpeace spokesperson but it is considerably threatened by his later 'countering' remark that impartiality is impossible. B's interest in seeing impartiality striven for is partly strategic (people expect it, so you have to look as if you're providing it) and partly a belief in the rightness of 'argument-testing' rather than unrestrained advocacy.

Finally, the group's own anti-nuclear position is reflected in comments which address the possibilities for the programme to be more effectively negative in its address, as in the following remark concerning visual effectiveness:

A. I think they could have done.. with a lot more on the environment. They did a bit about the lake and they had this idyllic lake with all this mist coming off the top which was nuclear reactive steam and, I mean, they could have done a good thing on that, pulled it out a bit longer.

2. Energy – The Nuclear Option

The initial response to this programme is one which registers its character as a promotional item – 'it was like a lengthened advert for BNFL' – and generally rejects its terms of reference:

D. It was clever sticking somebody who is supposed to be like an investigative journalist like Brian Walden... on these programmes that question politicians, and then allow him to go and ask questions that have obviously been prepared by the CEGB. It's a con.

Speaker C, as before, employs a civic framing, registering that this second programme includes material omitted, perhaps intentionally, from the first – instancing the programme's view that nuclear power may in the future be a necessity. Other speakers however are not prepared to accept these pro- nuclear arguments on the programme's word alone. It is too suspect as a source of authoritative knowledge.

Such dissatisfaction with the discursive terms within which *Energy – The Nuclear Option* handles the necessity/benefit/risk relationship is widespread among group members, some of whom, in seeing the programme's address to the viewer as unacceptable, relate its intentions and origins directly to 'government':

B. I'm saying, no, it wouldn't really have impressed anybody. It certainly wasn't their best...government people are very good at putting arguments over, that was a very poor show. What he did was tell you..make very clear,categoric statements and it was as if it was.. 'I know and I'm telling you' and people don't like being undermined like that, I don't think, no matter what political fence they sit on.

They speculate that the programme is designed with a view to 'getting us all lined up for privatisation'.

The group objects to the 'patronising' and 'condescending' tone of the presenter, and also register cynicism about his role as the 'impartial' investigator:

D. Then for him to start asking him all these tough questions when he was actually asking the guy who was paying his wages...

B. I think he (Marshall) wrote the questions.

A. The way he answered the questions quickly without thinking about them just proved he had been given them in advance or maybe even wrote them you know.

The group is also like other groups in finding the reassurances which Lord Marshall offers in this interview either unconvincing or productive of greater levels of anxiety, as in this comment – which also reflects more generally on the 'boomarang' effect of the emphasis on safety in this latter phase of the programme:

> B. *As long as you didn't ask any questions, it didn't make you think of another question... I mean all he's saying is 'an eight foot solid concrete block encased in another four foot solid concrete block' – so big deal we know we can get blown off the face of the earth... The guy at the end actually sort of showed the contradiction because the bit about Chernobyl, he said it blew a ten by ten square yard concrete block and so you knew...it just made him look like a block of concrete.*

Like most of our groups, this group registers a considerable gap between communicative intentions and communicative effectiveness. Yet speaker C remarks on the way in which the sequence of screenings serves to 'prime' the group to be more critical, thereby noting as significant in the second programme certain omissions to do with health risk and waste disposal which 'people in the street' might not notice or ('unprimed') be so sharply concerned about.

3. From Our Own Correspondent

Three key themes, not unique to this group, feature in their response to this item: a level of confusion about the status of what is depicted; a registering of the distinctively low-budget, and in some ways unsatisfactory, character of the 'production values', and the nature of the main appeal as being to do with emotions and human empathy:

> D. *A small-scale* Threads [Mid-80s BBC drama-documentary on nuclear war], *a smaller budget.*

> B. *A victim's view of it.*

> C. *I thought it was tacky myself, you didn't know what was real.*

> A. *Right at the beginning, I thought it was showing something that had really happened. It quite frightened me in a way. It was good for a low budget film.*

> C. *I thought it was difficult to trust the information that was in it.I don't know what to believe and what not to believe. The programme-makers were coming from a definite side. It wasn't really based on hard fact, whatever that is...*

With the exception of C (see below), the group finds that both the critical ideas behind the programme and their realization in a dramatic human narrative are quite acceptable. This dominantly positive reading nevertheless finds an obstacle to comprehension in the programme's design as an item which *appears* initially to be about Chernobyl:

> A. *It's like reinforcing the view that even the Russians said it would never happen in their industry and it happened...It confused me as well, at the beginning, with*

Chernobyl and this Russian presenter. And I suddenly heard 'Hartlepool' and I thought 'hang on, that's not in Russia' you know, that confused me for about a couple of seconds.

Elements of confusion remain, after the screening. When one speaker says: 'If it had been people from Chernobyl, then that would've probably been the most effective' he seems to be missing the point of the programme, to alarm a British audience with an imagined British disaster. Perhaps surprisingly, it is C who defends the approach taken whilst criticising the execution. For others, the confusion remains as something which the programme should *not* have produced, even for tactical reasons.

The programme's status as a narrative fiction seems to make the identification of bias less obvious a 'move' for viewers to make, a point we have noted elsewhere. The reasons for this, and for the countering it receives, are instructive:

D. It wasn't biassed though, because it took ordinary people who aren't involved in the planning decisions that go on or the management of the plant. All they're doing is living their lives and they've been affected. So she wasn't coming with any bias you know, her family had been affected by it, she'd lost her home...

C. I think it was biassed because they put forward a scenario that the nuclear industry doesn't even recognise as existing.

B. It probably had a tinge of bias but you didn't notice it because it was ordinary people talking who aren't in Greenpeace, who aren't involved in fighting against nuclear energy, who aren't involved in sitting on a board deciding what goes on. Just like – people.

D and B appear to ground the innocence of the programme in the perceived innocence of its central character, a naturalizing move which then places the *motivated* nature of narrative structure, characterisation and enactment – the positions behind the fiction – beyond inquiry. C radically departs from this precisely by seeing the scenario itself as a projected 'given' (the constructed hypothesis of a 'they') which the industry itself would deny. Whether one agrees with it or not, its commitment to a contested position makes it impossible to see as 'balanced', though for C the real issue may be the way in which its depictions *disguise* its commitment – here by dramatic naturalism rather than by assumed journalistic neutrality. (It is worth noting that to most likely viewers of this tape in the domestic or group settings intended by its producers, the probability of its having strong political preferences structured into its items would be rated as high *and* perfectly acceptable).

Summary

This group in general uses a strong political framing to makes sense of and assess the items which are watched. Within this frame, considerable suspicion of government-related institutions and spokespersons is manifested, making respondents sceptical of accounts from within the industry, however eminent the source. There is a stronger declared value attached to the testimony of 'ordinary people' than is found in many other groups and a related concern with assessing the benefits and risks question at this level too. The members of the group have anxieties both about the broadly environmental risks attaching to nuclear energy production and about the possibilities of a Chernobyl-style disaster occurring in Britain. The concern for 'ordinariness' and the high level of doubt about safety make the group in many respects ideal viewers for the *Northern Newsreel* account but as we have seen this does not prevent an experiencing of confusion in watching the programme. As in other groups with developed political affiliations, the interplay between civic and political framings of interpretative activity, particularly with regard to bias and balance, often sets up tensions not only among group members but also within individual member's accounts. The rules for 'fair' television are seen as conventions to be respected (not exploited for persuasive purpose as is seen to be the case in *ENO*) but the committed pursuit of the truth is also regarded by some members as a journalistic imperative and the differing strengths of their own sense as to where the 'truth' lies is often the source of variant readings and assessments. Speaker C, as we have noted, is far more committed than the others to viewing the programmes within terms of a model of 'balanced' exposition. Given the concern with bias which develops in relation to the first two programmes, we have noted how it is of interest that the text with which this group aligns most closely, *From Our Own Correspondent*, escapes from a charge of bias not by a counter-argument justifying committedness but by a shift to the level of the fictional characterisation, and of the political innocence therein depicted.

Heysham Nuclear Power Station Group

(This group consisted of five men)

1. Uncertain Legacy

This group strongly supported the nuclear industry. So it is not surprising that they are highly critical of *Uncertain Legacy*, perceiving it as hostile and therefore reacting, in civic terms, to its 'bias'. Where they can, they expose the illegitimacy of this, as entailing *mis*representation:

> A. Well if I was you know Joe Bloggs, a member of the public and I didn't know anything about the nuclear industry then I would be so against nuclear power now that it's just

not true. *I'd be moving to Sweden, or wherever. It's as silly as that. I'll give you a forinstance. It started off earlier on about Traws, that's the station with the lake, and its an early morning scene with the mist rising off the water, you know, and it's saying, and this is, they're discharging thousands of gallons of radioactive effluent into this lake which then gives you the immediate impression, and the high temperature, you know, that this was radiation and contamination sort of floating off the surface of the lake, an eerie, you know, sort of scary thing. It failed to say that the temperature was raised simply by the fact that you extract water from it, pass it through a turbine which is red hot turning steam back into water and it goes back into the lake, and that raises the temperature, it doesn't get anywhere near nuclear power, the nuclear side at all. But it failed to tell you that.*

For another speaker:

B. *There was no counter-arguments, it was all on the black side of things.*

B, unlike A, seems to have some difficulty in simply *rejecting* the reality of the 'black side' as presented in the programme. A's use of 'insider' knowledge in his critique here is very specific. Elsewhere, the group settle for a weaker rejection strategy, which less well-informed groups used too – they talk about domains of evidence not explored by the programme, which might (though they can't be sure) weaken its critical thesis:

C. *I think perhaps there is some concern about the leukaemia, but not necessarily, I think it wants examining....*

B. *That was something that they never compared against other areas with high instances of leukaemia that are away from nuclear power stations. They were all just on a concentrated area round the power stations.*

C. *I would have thought that if there was an actual link they should be surveying the actual people that work in the power stations, because surely we must be getting a fractionally higher dose than what the people are outside.....*

B. *that's right*

C. *..so there would be a higher case for leukaemias but they never mentioned that, you know. We'd be dropping like flies according to statistics that they were putting over.*

There is a tendency in this passage and elsewhere to take comfort in the inconclusiveness of the cancer/radiation arguments. If the critics haven't proved their case, if there is evidence that weakens the force of the known correlations, then the industry need not worry. They begin with the worry (see above) and then 'talk it down' in this way. They cannot substitute certainty for *Uncertain Legacy's* uncertainty, so they resist the terms of its final question.

Their concern for 'balance' at times shifts to an interpretative position which asks 'how do we come out of it, how could we have come out of it better'?

C. I think that's it, its the way you pitch it, isn't it? If he's talking on television [Lord Marshall] and that television programme's going out to the public, I think he's got to get down to something like their level, otherwise he's going to make no sense. And I think that's the way you tackle the question

D. The point he made was that there's that much radioactivity in your own garden, the amount that the nuclear industry sends out is negligible

Interviewer. You think that was a good point, did he put that across?

C. I think people understand things like that, yes.

A. I think if it had been backed up by the commentator saying things in favour, not in favour cause obviously he was so much against, but if he in fact spoke alongside Marshall on this type of thing and said 'yes this is perfectly true, these are, this is actually what is happening now' instead of having one man in isolation trying to put a case over in the few seconds that he's given. If it'd been backed up by the commentator being unbiased and saying 'this is indeed true'. You know. It was not that. It was all, as I say, fifty odd minutes against, and a few minutes for.

The 'you' in C's first contribution suggests a virtual identification by this speaker with Marshall's opportunities and obstacles as a participant in the programme. This contrasts with other passages where the impersonal 'you' seems to refer not to an industry advocate, but to a hypothetical, and open-minded, viewer:

B. But it was all, it was too one-sided, it was all one-sided. I mean if it, for a good interesting debate, argument you've got to have both sides and be able to get both sides into perspective and see both sides, you know, and make your own conclusions. That tried to make conclusions for you.

2. Energy – The Nuclear Option

The group is much more favourably disposed towards this programme, although initially seeing it as having a 'bias' that runs the opposite way to that of the first programme. Importantly, they perceive it as less manipulative because more factual:

A. So from that point... I mean, you know, it's not trying to gloss over the fact that radiation and contamination is dangerous. It wasn't biassed that way, it was biassed in the fact that it was saying that the way we build reactors and design them, and its as safe as anything could possibly be, you know, of that kind of thing. The other film dealt with, you know, hidden things that lurk in the night, you know, the mists.

They support the pro-industry conclusions of the programme, and they want to believe that it has achieved those conclusions by journalistically fair means. They do not percieve an illegitimate use of *Weekend World* as a model though they recognise Walden and read the interview sequence in terms of the normative principles of broadcast current affairs interviews:

B. He tried to ask the questions that ordinary people, Joe Public would ask.

Groups critical of *Energy – The Nuclear Option* generally identify a pretence at this point: Walden asks questions *scripted for him*, the point of which is to give Marshall the opportunity to give reassuring answers. Such groups don't usually find these answers very satisfactory! Not only does this group overlook the possibility of pretence, but it also approves of Marshall and his answers here.

C. Yes but, the thing was, they took his replies as, they were positive replies weren't they? rather than negative, I mean, the first one. They gave him the question about the leukaemia which I thought was a good one, and he mentioned the fact that there were pockets of leukaemia in areas that had no nuclear installations round them, and, whereas in the first one, obviously the chap was trying to dig out that wherever you build one there's problems.

3. From Our Own Correspondent

The group's initial disgust at the bias of this item is quickly worked into a critique of its approach as an offence against rationality:

A. Well it was so biassed, I mean, you know, absolutely unbelieveable, totally biassed one way that you know, I mean, even the people who were anti nuclear must think, look at that and think 'well that is a bit over the top'...

B. It was scaremongering, that's ...

C. If the idea was to hit headlines or produce television that would provoke argument, then that's the type of thing that does it.

Later in the discussion the political motivation behind the production is explored:

A. It's highly political isn't it. It's really just a political group, rather than the general public, is that sort of thing.

Like the Conservative group they represent it as so extreme in character as to have violated norms of legitimacy at least for the purposes of broadcast transmission.

C. But its frightening that that could go out to release. That's what frightens me; it's been made and it's for general release to the public.

C's fears do not prevent him from concurring in the group appreciation of the programme's entertainment value, and expressing good-humoured appreciation of its merits on its own anti-nuclear terms, merits of argument (the reduction of the evacuation zones) and merits of presentation.

C. You couldn't go back for your possessions, everything had to be left behind, it was just up and away. And then you was housed in camps, which I thought that was good as well (laugh) (?) these big wooden huts, and 'this is like, your new home for ...'

As with other groups, some confusion is admitted. One speaker *may* be register-ing an interpretation of the 'disaster at Hartlepool' scenario as a falsehood rather than an intended fiction.

> *A. No, they were just piling on the agony weren't they really? They were saying, you know, in spite of all this that's happened, they're still reducing the limits etcetera, you know, of evacuation, which makes it to appear far worse. That's presuming that the thing happened at Hartlepool anyway in the first place.*

Summary

This group's concern with the validity of fact and argument derives mainly from their very clear sense of themselves as insiders with access thereby to truths about the industry not possessed by the general public or by certain sorts of experts, namely journalistic 'experts' like the presenter of *Uncertain Legacy*. We have indicated the limitations of this privileged knowledge standpoint as these are manifest in the group's ongoing talk. Speaker B seems to represent the group at its most nervous in respect of the risk question; Speaker A contributes a distinc-tive focus upon (illegitimate) rhetorical mobilization of nonpropositional meanings.

These evidential interests are worked in relation to civic concerns, so that weak, false and tendentious arguments and facts correlate with 'bias': at a general level this is even-handed (both *Uncertain Legacy* and *Energy – The Nuclear Option* are biassed) but the group's identification with the industry reveals its strength in relation to the latter: they not only read with the grain of the programme's rhetoric (Walden asks challenging questions at the end of the film) but also approve the arguments given in reply (you do find leukaemia clusters wherever you look) – unlike every other group interviewed.

Their hostile response to the third item as a politicization of the issue takes them beyond the givens of TV practice into a fundamental querying of its legitimacy as public communication.

Friends of the Earth

(This group consisted of two men and three women)

1. *Uncertain Legacy*

In the initial stages of the discussion there is a strong emphasis upon the strengths and weaknesses of argument and the relation of these to the known and knowable facts. This is articulated with a concern for civic propriety, as in the following:

A. I thought it started off quite weakly, in that a lot of facts came out, various comments and statements made, but there was no sort of, you weren't, there was no real evidence, he didn't really go into the figures that were coming out.

It may have been, at times, I think, people might have thought it was rather reactionary and, you know, done from an anti-nuclear standpoint. ...To me, looking at it, it didn't seem a very balanced programme.

The 'real evidence' which for this respondent is missing is presumably evidence more conclusively anti-nuclear than what is actually presented – he does not want to learn that the risks are 'uncertain', he wants to learn that they are *real*. For him, then, the programme may be unbalanced in the sense that it is too ready to mount a critique of the industry on weak facts. However, there is also possibly a tension here – between the desire for truth and the approval of 'balanced inquiry' – of a kind which we noted in a number of groups.

In this phase, a strong if isolated assertion of positive personal response is made by one of the group, who is consistent throughout the session in insisting upon the validity of the 'gut feeling' as the basis for deciding issues and evaluating programmes.

D. It appealed to me a lot actually because I think they were just appealing to very basic fears, not particularly good facts but just people's basic fear instinct. I'm not very well up on the facts and so on of nuclear, but I know basically I'm scared of it, you know, and that's how it came across to me. I thought it was great.

However, despite their commitment to environmentalism, the group spend some time exposing the rhetorical effects of the programme as instances of *anti-nuclear bias*, as when one of them compares the presenter's framing of Goffman (the scientist critical of the nuclear industry) with his framing of Lord Marshall:

B. When he was asking people in the nuclear industry, people like Marshall, he was, like, biting wit (?) whereas when he was interviewing Goffman, he just took what he said as gospel, he didn't attempt any sort of critical questioning of him, which, well, he (?) with the other people he just sort of mocked what they were saying.

One speaker in particular recurrently evaluates the programme in displaced terms – its merits for her depend upon (her judgment of) its possible impact on others – since she does not need persuading that the industry is a problem. Her comments in the quotation which follows indicate that she is thinking initially of the open-minded uninformed viewer and then, after the interviewer's intervention, of the pro-nuclear viewer:

C. Well I think it would've increased people's distrust of the industry, it showed there were so many unanswered questions. But again, I did feel that the interviewer was obviously anti- the nuclear industry, so that ...

Interviewer. In the way that...?

C. The way he posed questions and that sort of thing.

Interviewer. Did you think that was something that in a sense flawed the programme or was a problem for you?

C. Not for me, but I feel that if I was pro the industry, I would think. 'Oh, this', you know, 'set up, they're asking the right questions, so that it shows the worst side of the industry rather than giving a fair crack of the whip to both sides'.

The group's consideration of the programme reflects a strong concern for credibility of argument, albeit displaced in some cases on to the credibility of particular 'expert' contributors. As the talk progresses, though, it is more and more the pro-nuclear position which comes under attack.

Speaker D, who responds in such strongly personal terms at the outset of the discussion, later combines a personal response with a kind of 'global fundamentalism' (i.e., protection of 'the planet' without reference to any specific human societies that are to benefit or to lose from its protection). We illustrate this here, not because it is an integral part of Friends of the Earth's discourse but rather because it is (perhaps surprisingly) infrequently in evidence in this discussion and entirely missing from the accounts of any other groups:

D. Well like I said, he was interviewing the way I would have liked to have done, because I don't know an awful lot, I just go by my instinct, and I know that it's too much for this small planet, that's how I feel, just, you know, so it made me feel a bit better, the (?) programme, it helped me stay as I am with my views. It didn't influence me towards nuclear in any way whatsoever. It's not natural, you know, so ....

2. Energy – The Nuclear Option

C. He was very much pro-nuclear, wasn't he, as if he was presenting the government's case, the industry's case. Extraordinarily dogmatic view, patronising view.

A civic frame once again generates the first response and is pursued in that the group recognises and criticises the programme's pro-nuclear bias. Environmental concerns are more to the fore however. In particular, planetary interests are still on the agenda for D, but this time giving her a more propositional (and political) 'handle' for her criticism:

D. Also, he said about... there'd been no accident in Britain, as if we're not one world. Doesn't matter if it's over in Russia or somewhere

A critical account of the programme's discussion of alternative energy sources is also mounted:

A. It was just taken as read that energy demand in the country was going to rise, that was good for the country, it was almost the case that, 'the more electricity we consume the more profitable we are as a nation' and it totally glossed over that. It glossed over anything about how much energy savings could benefit. ... The only things it, the only opposite things it – well, it was coal, which it didn't want for political reasons – the miner's strike was obviously to the fore. Or that it was going to run out. We had a few windmills, and then a few ..., possibility of a barrage, and tidal power, but there was no mention of solar power, or geothermal energy, or producing methane from waste, so it glossed over quite a lot of other alternatives.

A also remarks that neither of the two programmes deals with the effects of radiation on things other than human beings, extending even urther the universalism of green consciousness:

A. It didn't say anything about the environmental effects of radiation on things other than humans. Having said that I'm not sure the other programme did either. It was only concerned with the environmental effects on people wasn't it? It didn't sort of say what the effect would be on other forms of life.

Other members of the group are ready to give credit where they feel it due,in keeping with their general disposition towards 'evenhandedness':

C. They really homed in on the safety thing didn't they ... It's obviously a thing they feel very confident about.

Interviewer. Do you think that was good then?

C. Yes, yes

A. I think we can understand it a bit better how it works.

Interviewer. Did you think as a consequence of that it was safer?

B. The safety bits, the interlocks and all that, that came over very well.

This can be read in two ways, giving rather different identities to C's 'they'. Perhaps both meanings are operative. On the one hand, it reads as a somewhat illogical *conflation* of praise for the programme's presentation of plant safety and praise for the industry's arrangements to ensure plant safety – illogical because if the real reason for their satisfaction is a new conviction that plants are safe they should be praising the industry for that, not the programme. But on the other hand, these two judgments reflect a perfectly rational understanding that if they found themselves convinced by that part of the programme, then the programme deserves credit for convincing them. Deconstruction of the programme's rhetorical structure and devices is pursued with some enthusiasm, with particular reference to the imitation of *Weekend World* that it attempts:

A. The way he started it, he started it just like he starts Weekend World *with 'Good Evening' or whatever it was, like he was just doing that, like it was just that sort of presentation.*

Their critique of this aspect is sharpened in considering the role of Brian Walden as presenter, which they return to several times in the discussion. Eventually they appear to concur in thinking that the Walden device does not work (after one speaker has praised his 'professionalism', and another objected to his patronising and dogmatic tone)

> B. He's somebody that the public sees as impartial so to use him in a partial setting I don't think really works.

3. *From Our Own Correspondent*

The group broadly approves of this item and does not spontaneously query the legitimacy of its approach, even though it notes the special power of an *imaginative* appeal. On some topics, shock tactics are seen to be a proper way of starting a debate:

> D. It's definitely visual. It brings it back, into your backyard.

Later, the same speaker reflects on the usefulness of the item:

> D. I think it was useful, yes, to people who don't know an awful lot, who don't want to know an awful lot about statistics and so on, to get to just normal people, everyday people [The speaker here compares the item to the mid 80s BBC drama-documentary on nuclear war, Threads, noting how this 'shocked everyone']. And that's similar – very mild version. But that's the sort of thing that does get to people.

Despite accepting the power and legitimacy of 'What if...', there is emphasis too on the 'point' of the item – reappropriating it for rational purposes. Its point is perceived to be that a Chernobyl *scale* accident is possible in the U.K. Some disagreement is expressed on the merits of mentioning the comparatively small-scale but actual Hartlepool accident – the speaker who believes that it was right to mention that accident does so on grounds which indicate that he is operating standards of propriety in which it is appropriate to treat honestly and openly the arguments of the 'other side'. The counter-argument that he is sensitive to is the one that says a Chernobyl-type accident is not possible in Britain:

> B. I think the point did need to be made, [about the real accident at Hartlepool] otherwise you could just leave it at 'well, Chernobyl happened', because the point has been stressed over and over by the government that 'it can't happen here'. That particular accident can't but other accidents can, or maybe can.

Summary

The group responded to the lack of balance in both of the first two programmes but, as noted above, in their account of *From Our Own Correspondent* the question of bias is scarcely raised. This pattern seems to tie in with group dynamics, in the following way. Although all speakers contribute to the civic framing with the exception of D, it seems to be *driven* (introduced, and led) by the male speakers. It is in the contributions of the male speakers that 'civic' criticism gets its most detailed articulation with talk about the strengths and weaknesses of argument. When it comes to the third programme there is agreement (at least superficially) that it has only one main point: *that* point (the possibility of a nuclear power disaster in Britain) provokes, again, a concern for fairness in televisual argumentative practice. The male speakers focus on this concern, but for the group as a whole the item provokes considerations much broader than the balance/bias issue.

PHASE TWO

The following three groups are the ones which viewed a single programme, one edition of *Heart of the Matter*.

Women's Institute

(This group consisted of seven women)

It is a strong framing around the personal, rather than a concern with the conventions of public debate, which here provides the primary line of engagement and comprehension. This empathetic response can be seen right at the beginning of the discussion, as the plight of the mother whose child is afflicted with leukaemia is recognised:

> A. *We realise what a terribly anxious time it is for parents, and they must be really out of their minds, watching their children you know, grow up and get to a certain age and they realise, you know, that there's something wrong...*

This is a theme returned to in attempts to make sense of the uncertainties surrounding the proof and probability question, as well as providing a point of comparison against other people in the programme who they feel are uncaring. In this way the industry is seen as big and powerful, trying to 'cover up' the truth about the dangers of radiation against the interests of 'an ordinary working person....on her own' who in their eyes stands very little chance if any of winning the law suit. In fact so dominant is the personal frame that ultimately their sympathetic identification and interest in the domestic situation overrides the difficulties presented by the programme's attempt to articulate the key terms of scientific and legal dispute.

The specific character of the risk depicted, childhood leukaemia, together with a belief that irrefutable proof is essential to the success of a law suit, lead to questioning of the programme's account in terms of gaps in the information it provides:

B. I just wonder how if it's affecting children, how is it not affecting people, well, working directly with it. And you know it just makes you wonder how it's just the children that the programme's about, it doesn't mention anyone else there catching it, does it?

Interviewer. What sort of evidence will they give though?

B. Well they'll have to have positive proof, won't they, that its causing that ?

C. You mean the family ?

B. Or the solicitor, whoever's agreed to it ... they'll have to have positive proof otherwise they can just close.

Interviewer. Didn't they say that in this type of case they can have a high probability rather than proof ?

D. Well I don't see how they'd win it without positive proof.

C. I can't see it either.

Nevertheless, their final interpretation is that leukaemia *is* caused by radiation (they are convinced by the editor of *Radiation and Health* because he comes across to them as the most confident speaker) though they would have preferred more medical information, more facts:

B. How does it affect in other countries? Is the rate of leukaemia high there where they have the same workings going on ?

A. What is the situation away from Sellafield, I mean, have they had a survey in the hospitals all over the country?

Their lack of satisfaction with the clarity of the programme's expert testimony (and, indeed, its own expositional discourse) is also evident in the discussion of the 'turns' in the direction of evidence given by just one of the contributors:

Interviewer. So what do you think the conclusion of the programme is?)

E. Well its hard to say, isn't it? One chap was saying it did (radiation did cause leukaemia), and then he was contradicting himself. That was that professor.

B. Well, the professor did seem to think it came from that, didn't he?

E. He said it didn't at first and then he sort of changed it.

C. He hadn't proved it. He said it could cause it and it couldn't cause it...

The group as a whole want to put their faith in an expert and want that expert to deliver clear answers. When these cannot be given they are uncertain how to proceed. The editor of *Radiation and Health*, however, succeeds in getting his message across and the plight of the mother gives a human force to what he says.

The personal feelings and own experiences of the group may at times appear to obstruct their path to understanding the terms preferred by the programme but they also seem to provide their primary channel of engagement with its account. For example, talk around whether or not radiation from Sellafield is the cause of leukaemia leads to talk on local pollution from a chemical plant, traffic pollution and toxic waste, which then turns *back* into a questioning of whether Sellafield can be blamed for the leukaemia.

To this extent the *details* of the programme are not registered. Indeed reference to the programme's argument are few and invariably turn on the problems of uncertainty. The major thrust of interpretation comes from the personal appeal within the programme and personal experiences external to it. The 'ifs and buts' of probabilistic argument in a situation where conclusive proof is either extremely hard or impossible to obtain are generally perceived as inadequacies. As indicated, the group's discussion tends to hover at the surface of the programme, preferring what they 'know' and thus feel most comfortable with as subjects for discussion, rather than following closely a narrative progression which seems to imply a causal link whilst also introducing information which could be used as evidence to the contrary. Just it is an empathy with the mother which forms the begininings of their assessment, so it is the situation of her fighting alone which finally provides them with a 'conclusion' – morally, she should win her case, but they consider this doubtful due to the lack of hard proof, and to the sheer scale, influence and resources of the nuclear industry. The personal framing leads through to an implicit anti-nuclear stance, but one which only in part follows the anti-nuclear cues in the programme's exposition.

Arts Students

(This group consisted of two men and two women)

The group's initial responses made it clear that they understood the programme to be addressing a dilemma – that between the Sellafield plant as a major employer in the area and the possible health risks that this might entail. Each member saw the programme delivering a quite clear judgement on the central issue, for example:

> A. *I just think they make it really obvious that it does cause leukaemia.*

Comment of this kind invites a consideration of whether the projecting of such a clear 'message' constitutes a problem of imbalance and bias. As we have noted in our earlier group accounts, a concern with the propriety of debate features significantly in most discussions at some point or other, and often right at the start. Speaker A believes that *Heart of the Matter* supports the idea of a link between Sellafield radiation and leukaemia but that this is, in fact, likely to be the *truth.* It cannot, therefore, be seen as 'partial opinion', despite its being contested by a number of programme participants. Others feel that the programme attempts an objectivity which leaves the viewers free to make up their own minds. At the same time, they regard the account as being unequal in representation – there were fewer people interviewed who supported the side of the industry. One speaker adds a comment about the inevitability of a degree of 'bias' in a programme of this kind:

> B. *I think it was certainly trying to be fair, I mean the formula of the programme, it has to be fair doesn't it ? That's the idea of it, to present you with the arguments and you make your choice, but obviously the people making it have to have some bias somewhere, and I think that necessarily comes through.*

The group's response to the perceived 'imbalance' in the representation of the pro-industry case resembles that put forward by some respondents in our Phase One study, insofar as it is undecided whether or not the cause is *programme* bias or weaknesses in the pro-industry position. Certainly, when respondents discuss the contribution made to the programme by the spokesman for BNFL they find fault with his televisual presentation 'he came across as really pompous') and also with the substance of his arguments:

> A. *That man, you know, the one that was representing Sellafield, he did have his fair say, but his arguments were really weak and just bullshit really, honestly.*

> C. *He came out with some stuff which was just total crap, he was just like trying to weakly defend it, like when he said 'this is not true' and quickly gave a back up of an organisation.*

> D. *And like he was saying why in the middle of summer on the hottest day, the beach is empty and he said 'well this isn't Blackpool,' it was just laughable.*

> B. *I mean 'this is a scarcely populated area'! I mean Scotland is a scarcely populated area but you know they have tourists there.*

> D. *From what I could gather he was sort of blaming leukaemia at one point on a sudden influx of people...*

The scorn and level of disagreement with the BNFL account suggests, of course, a strong predisposition against nuclear energy. Perhaps not suprisingly therefore, the group sees the contrasting testimony and arguments of the editor of *Radiation and Health* as 'really persuasive' and 'interesting and succinct'. One respondent notes a strategic parallelling of the two speakers:

> B. *...they set him up as the equivalent of the information person from Sellafield and I thought that worked very much in his favour.*

The depiction of Mrs. D'Arcy and her daughter are important to the group's interpretation. There is a recognition of an emotional appeal but this is seen as controlled ('they didn't dramatize that') as well as effective. The visual rhetoric of the programme is credited with impact in the same way – shots of Gemma D'Arcy in the paddling pool, the empty beach and the power station situated amongst the 'idyllic' countryside are cited.

Whereas the strength of Mrs D'Arcy's contribution ('she is...the one that sways people') is seen to follow both from the awfulness of her experience and her position as 'ordinary' ('she was, like, a real person'), Professor Doll's views receive respect on the grounds of his being an 'eminent scientist' and behaving as such:

> A. ..*he had a bit more sort of technical authority than the rest of them, it was like he was the intellectual, so he was the one whose point of view you had to take and because he was a scientist he was probably unbiassed ... so you could accept most of what he said.*

Doll's account of the probabilities involved in assessing the risk factor is one which most respondents find hard to follow. Interestingly, they note their expectation that he would *confirm* the link between radiation and the leukaemias, thus fitting into a pattern of assessment which they have discerned in the programme by that point. When he states that such a direct link is unlikely, the result is a degree of confusion. Discussion of this leads to reflections on the programme's conclusions and the way they hinge on probabilities.

> B. *You really get the impression that you cannot deny that it is something to do with Sellafield. Then again you get the feeling that you might not ever be able to prove it.*

This, they feel, means that success in the courts is unlikely, and particularly so given their belief that courts are, in any event, inclined favourably towards Government interests.

Chemistry Students

(This group consisted of three men and two women)

The first impression of the programme voiced by this group was a unanimous criticism of its vagueness. As they amplify this point it becomes clear that the central element of their dissatisfaction is the inconclusiveness of the arguments, registered as an absence of 'solid facts':

> A. ...*I got part of the way through and I began to get bored of it, because it wasn't telling me anything, there's no facts and I didn't pay too much attention to what people said. I just took the general idea, the general idea was that there's a little girl with leukaemia and there's a big company and they're fighting about it. You know obviously the person that did the programme is biassed towards the little girl. And I wasn't going to get any facts from it.*

They do not, on their own account, interrogate whether the evidence reviewed supports any particular conclusion, even probabilistically. This may indicate a desire to keep themselves at a sceptical distance in the face of an unresolved dispute. Notwithstanding this distanciation from the arguments, they are prepared to give their endorsement to Professor Doll – 'you don't get to that sort of standard without knowing what you're talking about', whose position they are prepared to accept because of his eminence, rather than from any more direct evaluative engagement with what he says.

This recognition that the programme's propositional discourse does not resolve the issue one way or the other is complemented by a perception that it has an emotional structure which favours one side, as the above quotation shows. Their reaction to the existence of this emotional structure is a critical one – they believe it is illegitimate in such a programme, which should strive for objectivity. Perceiving that the bias favours the 'victim', not the industry, initially elicits from them denials of their own vulnerability to its emotional appeal, but later they admit the effectiveness of that appeal upon them:

C. *It influenced you a lot because it kind of centres around family unity and it kept referring to Gemma D'Arcy and you know, she's a dead sweet kid, and you think 'oh its really sad'.*

E. *And they showed her when she said something about, 'if I don't get the bone marrow will I die ?' ... its a bit of a tear jerker that sort of thing.*

These comments contain elements which reflect their understanding of the programme's intention to achieve these effects as well as admissions that the intention has succeeded – though not to the extent of producing in them the conviction that the D'Arcy's case is a sound one which, therefore, ought to win in court. They seem to suspect what they see as a further programme intention to influence the viewers' judgement on this count.

They interpret the bias of the programme not only as a consequence of the foregrounding of this powerfully affective personal tragedy to attract the 'sympathy vote', as it were, but also as a bias which is manipulatively reinforced at the visual level. BNFL are, they believe, 'made to look bad'. The industry spokesman contrasted with Mrs. D'Arcy is seen as a 'big shot' sitting complacently behind a desk :

C. ....*you expected to see someone with a big fat cigar in a minute – if you hadn't seen him it would have been better.*

What is more they think his lack of knowledge makes him sound as though he is covering up the real risk.

This group begin with a desire above all else for facts. They try at points to differentiate themselves from other viewers, more vulnerable to the emotional appeal, and their affiliation to a scientific discipline may be responsible for their conviction that knowledge is objective and attainable, and that the authority of an eminent scientist is to be trusted. They are also, however, reluctant to engage with the scientific arguments as these are presented in the programme – no mention is made, for instance, of the hypothesis that dose limits in Sellafield are too low, and the relevance of this hypothesis. Four of the group members do accept at the end of the discussion that the nature of this court case rests on probability not proof. They themselves would like to see Mrs. D'Arcy win her case on these terms. This suggests that despite their dissatisfaction with the programme on grounds of inconclusiveness, they feel some sympathy for its appeal. One speaker, A, holds himself somewhat apart from this group consensus. His stance is a defensive one – he refuses to develop much engagement with a programme basically unworthy because of its lack of straight facts and its emotionality.

OTHER GROUPS

In this section we shall look very briefly at the interpretations offered by other participating groups and individuals. In the space available it is not possible to provide full accounts of that material on a group-by- group basis. We have concentrated therefore upon trying to illustrate the range of responses to each of the three programmes in Phase One of the study (all of the Phase Two groups have been discussed above), in an attempt to bring out important similarities between these groups and others already considered as well as interesting differences, and even idiosyncracies:

1.Uncertain Legacy

Several groups confirmed to us the significance of the visual imagery and picked out the sequence shot at Trawsfynnedd Lake for particular comment:

(Women's discussion and action group)

I thought some of the visual shots were really quite powerful, you, know, the ones in the green field like 'This is England and here we have this horror looming on the side of the shore' or 'here we have a nice little lake, guess what's at the bottom of it?'

The speaker here does not contextualise the shots in terms of the programme's narrative progression, but instead evokes an 'unseen threat' strand of meaning by mentioning two visual expressions of that threat and projecting each of them into words, the imagined linguistic equivalents of those images. Another speaker from one of the mixed groups spoke of this sequence as 'lovely *Jaws* photography', whilst the following comment was made by a member of the SLD group in the context of discussing how visual images contributed towards the bias of the programme:[18]

(SLD group)

I think to a certain extent with the Trawsfynnedd thing, the fact that, they sort of sunk into the murky depths of the lake, it sort of made it seem a bit, well, dirty almost, and they were saying 'there is such and such a level of plutonium'

The tentativeness of this phrasing may be compounded of carefulness to get the description right, with caution in attributing intentionality to what is taken to be the general significance.

Most groups went through a moment in which they expressed the view that in some way or other, *Uncertain Legacy* favoured the anti-nuclear side of the argument, yet varied in their reactions to that perceived 'bias'. Thus, for instance:

(Mixed group 1)

I think it was an excellent film and I think it was biassed against nuclear fuel but I think that's what we need.

It is hardly bias as 'unfairness' which is being advocated here, but rather the legitimacy in broadcasting of taking a critical, investigative position. Yet it is interesting to see the term 'bias' being used in this context, suggesting once more the difficulty, within the civic frame, of separating fairness and truth-seeking as criteria of evaluation. Another speaker in the same group avoids the use of the term bias but makes essentially the same point:

(Mixed group 1)

It was a good programme, it was there to bring the nuclear industry into question and it did that very well.

In contrast, the SLD group seemed less satisfied with the approach:

(SLD group)

A. It felt a bit as though we were comparing apples and pears. It would've been interesting to have had the same type of people talking to or about the same things on a say, on a technical level.

B. I think the programme was slightly against the nuclear industry and I think if they wanted a more balanced programme they would've had some sort of discussion between scientists.

---

18 *This is a reference to the 1975 Hollywood disaster movie* Jaws, *featuring a predatory shark whose concealed threat to bathing holidaymakers set up terrifying associations around the ideas of surface and depth.*

On the one hand these speakers are clearly reacting negatively to the absence of formal markers of balance – balance as a procedural requirement. But at the same time, behind that concern with propriety of presentation, lies a substantive anxiety which the other group do not share – that there are scientifically-grounded arguments on the other side of the case which were improperly omitted from the programme. This inhibits the group from discussing what *is* presented.

So 'bias' for many of our respondents took the form of absences – here, it is the absence of scientists to represent the industry which is criticised. Lord Marshall of course is a scientist, yet, accessed in this programme in his capacity as chairman of the CEGB, he comes across to our groups primarily as a businessman. Elsewhere our groups articulated bias as manipulative imagery, as in the first of the SLD quotes above. Sometimes respondents produced quite complicated accounts of non-parallel treatments, as in the following (talking about the use of statistics in the programme):

(Women's discussion and action group)

But in fact they used them (statistics) quite cleverly, because they were talking about milliverts or whatever it was, and using statistical [data]....And that doesn't mean anything. But for the 'against' argument they were actually using the number of people that died, which is another statistic, but they're talking about it in human terms, which is far more relevant.

2. Energy – The Nuclear Option

More than one group found difficulties with this programme's attempt to present a favourable view of the nuclear industry in the framework of a current affairs documentary:

(Medical students group)

I thought it was more an advert than a discussion really. It was an advert by the electricity board saying 'nuclear power ....' well, they try to say that it's a discussion, but it isn't.

(Women's discussion and action group)

I kept expecting him to do the other side of it because he'd do that, for Weekend World, then you would've had more of the other side of the argument. I kept thinking, well he's going to come on to the other side now, and he never did.

Both of these quotations suggest that the *Weekend World* format has set up expectations of balance and open discussion, so that as the programme develops it is perceived as failing to deliver something it has itself 'promised' in virtue of adopting that format. There was, however, a speaker in one group for whom

Brian Walden's established reputation in broadcast television enhanced the credibility of a programme to which she had a favourable response:

(Mixed group 2)

I thought it was better than the first one because it showed the alternatives and the caring CEGB and they were saying 'we understand the problems with nuclear power and we're looking into other sources' and you get the feeling that they're not just throwing this dangerous product at you, they are looking at other things. It was better [than Uncertain Legacy]. And of course the fellow who was doing it, he does all the political programmes doesn't he? and you just take him as being a very honest chap who would only do the honest thing.

From the industry's point of view this would seem to represent an optimal response to the programme. Yet this kind of reading is rare – and even this speaker seems to be reflexively aware that Walden is being *used* to achieve the effect that has, in her case, been successful.

Mismatch between the programme's intentions and its effects takes a number of more specific forms as well as this general failure of the current affairs programme design. For example, there were several further instances of the 'boomerang' effect identified in the accounts above, whereby the emphasis upon plant safety eventually becomes so extreme as to heighten the anxiety viewers began with:

(Women's discussion and action group)

It's sort of counter-productive, so they kept talking about all these safety things, and safety things within safety things, and you thought, 'God, it must be bad because they've got that many safety things'. And then when that engineer was talking about the construction and how safe the construction of the actual building was, I suddenly started thinking about Ronan Point and places that had fallen down.

A different kind of mismatch between intention and effect can be seen in the following:

(Mixed group 1)

They just kept saying, you know, 'Frank Layfield', 'Frank Layfield', and then showed a picture of a book, it just seemed very disjointed in that way I thought.

In this case, the fact that the independent Layfield Report is being used in the programme as an authority for the industry's own conclusions about nuclear energy – that it is acceptably safe, that there really is a need for nuclear power, etc. – is not registered. The respondent has noted Layfield's salience for the programme but not what that salience consists in.

3. *From Our Own Correspondent*

Admissions of doubt about what this programme presents occur amongst these groups as amongst the groups we looked at in more detail above. In the following example it is the status of the final on-screen written text which is questioned:

(Individual respondent A)

But at the end, whether what I was reading was fact or not, because it, was make-believe all the way through, when it came up with the statistics at the end I didn't know if that was related to the film I was watching or if that was the policy.

This is an aspect of the general interpretative problem that *From Our Own Correspondent* poses for respondents with its fictionalizations, its surprise effects, and its articulations across different time/space locations. Some groups reject the approach, others react favourably:

(Medical students group)

Once I realised it was fictitious it lost its credibility, its impact, you know, because, you knew, I mean I knew it was just make-believe after that.

[Same speaker] I think it was meant to make us feel like, because it was British people, right, more at home, but in a way it did exactly the opposite, cause it wasn't real, so you just had a good laugh at it, you know.

This can be contrasted with statements from groups who appreciated the impact of the human story as credibly realistic – in one case, below, from someone with a comparable personal experience and in the other case, through imaginative projection:

(Women's discussion and action group)

I found it unpleasant because it reminded me of when the riots were on, [British urban riots of 1981], cause I actually lived right in the middle of it and I had to run away and leave my home and, you know, take my two children, like she did, and just literally run, we never had no coats, nothing, my two sons never even had a pair of shoes, this is in the middle of the night. And it was very emotional in parts, you know, it was really convincing, although I knew it was just a set up I thought it was done very well.

(SLD group)

I thought it was very interesting because I thought at first it was the result of some kind of Glasnost or something, and then suddenly 'Hartlepool'. It was a very clever way of going about it. And it did seem realistic, I can imagine that sort of thing happening, I mean, that's what appears to have happened after Chernobyl. I mean it wasn't a very long film, it didn't go into a lot of detail, but it did seem to cover things which happened at Chernobyl.

The 'glasnost' theme occurred to more than one person. It has to be abandoned, of course, once the realisation dawns that this is not a news report on Chernobyl, but it provoked an interesting use of the story's comparative potential on the part of one respondent who said:

(SLD group)

> Well actually, when it first started and I thought it was about, Chernobyl, I thought 'Oh wouldn't it be great if we had this sort of openness over here'. And I don't think we would, and the nuclear industry is infamous for its secrecy.

The speaker does not go on to draw the conclusion that one of the programme's intended messages concerns the secrecy of the British nuclear industry compared with the new openness of Soviet society – it is left as a 'private' inference, and since the Soviet news scenario is fictional, the warrant for the inference becomes hypothetical. Nevertheless, it is an interesting interpretative act, and one which the respondent himself found it worthwhile to mention, even after having relinquished it.

5   Variation and convergence

Introduction

In this chapter we approach the group accounts from a more comparative perspective. On the one hand, we have tried to identify aspects of interpretation and response which seem to us to be shared across all the accounts, albeit with different inflections according to the discursive context and the interpretative priorities of each group. On the other hand, we have tried to present analyses of the six Phase One accounts in such a way as to bring out as sharply as possible the differences between them, not so much in respect of particular programme characteristics but in their general orientation to the material screened. With this in mind this chapter has a section on *variation* and one on *convergence* – as well as a section, *dynamics of interpretation and response*, in which we go into more detail about the interpretative discourse itself.

The sections on convergence and on dynamics of response do not require any particular prefatory comment. The following remarks are concerned with the section on variation and explain how we have organised the material, and our reasons for doing it in that way. The *variation* section consists of three subsections. In each subsection we take two of the six Phase One groups and compare them. The pairings are: Labour and Conservative; the Rotary club and the unemployed; the Heysham workers and Friends of the Earth. The rationale for this approach is that two-way comparisons are easier to present than multiple comparisons. And of course the pairings have been chosen with some thought on our part as to the value of particular comparisons. The value of differing political allegiances, as in the Labour-Conservative contrast, is self-explanatory. In the case of the Rotary-Unemployed comparison, we were interested in exploring how a group of professional middle-class males with a strong official stake in the established social order would compare with a group whose unemployed status gave them no such official stake. In coming together as an organised group of unemployed people they can be seen as trying to create for themselves an oppositional social identity. The value of the Heysham/Friends of the Earth comparison was the potential it offered for exploring interpretative differences resulting from prior affiliations. The Heysham workers were affiliated *de facto* by their employment to the very industry under scrutiny. The Friends of the Earth group had an affiliation, through their organisation's policies, to the anti-nuclear side of the argument. In developing these contrasts we have again made use of the notion of *frame* as an analytic concept. Framing provides us with a scaffolding for the comparisons. We have indicated the use made by each group of the five frames previously identified as the most salient ones across all of the respondent ac-counts – the civic frame, the political frame, the evidential frame, the environmen-tal frame and the personal frame. A sixth frame – the formal frame – is also introduced. This allows us to identify more sharply and comparatively those moments in which groups give primary attention to the formal organisation of the screened material.

In this way we have been able to draw attention to some very significant variations. Different groups privilege different frames. A frame which is salient for one group is not so for another. The articulation of two or more frames is not the same across groups. It is at this level we begin to see the effect of a group's social identity upon their reactions to the programmes. The selection and orde-ring of these frames can be seen as an expression of the *agendas* which the groups bring to the interpretative task. We introduce this notion of agenda as a poten-tially useful analytic concept alongside that of frame. In this study, where the emphasis has been substantive rather than theoretical and the approach explor-atory,we have found it preferable to keep a light conceptual apparatus, in which both frame and agenda receive only provisional theorization.

Variation

1. The Conservative Party and the Labour Party

The discussions of these two groups are marked, as one might expect, by dif-ferences in general disposition towards nuclear energy. The Conservative group incline towards sympathetic consideration of the case for its continuation and development as government policy, the Labour group are deeply sceptical. Nevertheless, within the terms of this basic distinction, there are a suprising number of variations and the Labour group includes one member who clearly views the pro-nuclear case much more positively than other members. The Conservative group also displays considerable anxiety over current safety levels and over the question of the disposal of waste, so this is by no means a simple 'pro/con' contrast. A second (and related) distinction can be seen in contrasting emphases. First of all, there is the frustration recurrently articulated by the Conservative group as they note the absence of authoritative scientific opinion in the programmes, and the presence, variously, of presenter assessments, the projection of the industry's own 'corporate' view (most unsatisfactorily exemplified in Lord Marshall's contributions) and melodramatic alarmism. Such a search for the available underlying 'facts of the matter', together with an indication of how they might be *presumed* to favour the nuclear energy case, even if not conclusively, comes through in this comment about the desirability of:

(Conservative)

..some people who are involved and very knowledgeable debating with some people of anti-nuclear energy views.

Such an emphasis can be paired with the *tension* in the Labour group between a 'civic' acceptance of the need for balanced debate and a belief in the value of a weighted treatment in cases (like this) where the line-up of known facts is already, in their opinion, such as to count against an established position. A strongly naturalized version of this view of the available evidence comes through in the following remark:

(Labour)

I think the subject's so horrendous and the facts so frightening that we should see them as they are.

The Conservative viewers, too, sometimes have problems in achieving equilibrium between a desire both for 'fairness' (a central civic principle, of course) and for 'truth', but they hold to a different and less confident set of assumptions about the likely nature of the latter. Moreover, given this, they do not feel the urgency that members of the Labour group feel to influence public opinion (in the latter's case, to *change* it) by conscious persuasive strategy.

The emphases outlined above can also be related to the attitudes towards authority displayed by the groups – the Conservative group respectful (of the Layfield Report, the scientific community, Government policy) though severely critical of particular performances; the Labour group distrustful of the inter-connections between the nuclear lobby and political allegiance and more inclined to frame both 'evidence' and 'form' (in respect, say, of the probability/proof issue or of the conventions of commentary-over-film) as inherently problematic. Though the Conservative account is certainly not without its moments of cynicism ('there's not much honest information given') it stops well short of entertaining the negative scenario outlined in *From Our Own Correspondent*. This item is regarded not only as unsatisfactory in relation to the topic but as a *political* intervention of a kind which can only be responded to politically (by suggestions that it should be banned and the circumstances of its production investigated). For example:

(Conservative)

I know this is a democratic country but sometimes democracy goes too far here.

The Labour group, whilst noting certain deficiencies of execution in this piece, nevertheless generally approve of its thrust.

(Labour)

A. Oh, I enjoyed it, I thought it was good.

B. Yes, I enjoyed it.

A dislike of *Energy – The Nuclear Option* is, however, shared by both groups, bringing out formal framings most sharply – the identification of televisual devices and their motivations. Although the inflections of interpretation vary, there is a good deal of common ground to the problems perceived here by both groups under analysis (we discuss negative responses to this programme across the whole range of groups in a later section). This involves a suspicion of the integrity of professional advocacy ('he was being paid', Conservative; 'he gave the answers he thought we ought to be having', Labour) and a critical response to Lord Marshall's attempts at reassurance (a reading made of *Uncertain Legacy* as well as of the CEGB programme). The last point comes through stronger in the Conservative account ('...and in the next breath he said 'the top blew off of Chernobyl''), perhaps partly as a result of their greater degree of disappointment.

2. The Unemployed Group and the Rotary Club

An 'evidential' framing is more salient for the Rotarians than for the unemployed, but both groups suspect, even if they cannot dispute, presented evidence. Even truth claims overtly authored by the programmes can become suspect, as when the unemployed say of Walden's comments on the exhaustion of other fuel supplies that 'he never went to anyone outside the industry or anyone outside himself really' .The Rotarians are less specific. Both groups suppose, of *Energy – The Nuclear Option* and *Uncertain Legacy*, that other evidence could undermine the programme's stance. But the Rotarians warrant their suspicions by appeals to formal knowledge which they possess as professionals:

(Rotary)

My knowledge of the American legal system would lead me to believe, that the evidence produced around that Three-mile Island incident was actually counterproductive and made me less likely to believe the general thesis.

The evenhandedness of the suspicion also suggests a 'civic frame', with an impartiality requirement. Yet both groups find partiality legitimate and/or unavoidable. Speaker C (Unemployed) holds out for impartiality but eventually concedes its impossibility. This group (apart from C) reads the human story in *From Our Own Correspondent* as unbiased because experiential. For C the drama rests on the contentious point that a Chernobyl-type disaster could happen in

Britain. The Rotarians likewise recognise a 'point', made through emotionally compelling dramatization. They themselves resist the compulsion: the unemployed group less so:

(Unemployed)

Right at the beginning I thought it was showing something that had really happened. It quite frightened me in a way.

The only comparable 'personal' response from the Rotarians is a displaced one – the programme is not meant for their generation but for younger viewers.

The unemployed group more consistently than the Rotarians operates a 'political' frame. 'They' (industry-government) want to influence public opinion in favour of nuclear power and the interested basis of their case must always be kept in mind:

(Unemployed)

...they said beforehand that [Chernobyl] could never possibly happen, and it did, and they said again it could never happen and it did [Hartlepool] but right now they're saying it could never happen.

Only *Energy – The Nuclear Option* pushes the Rotarians into a similar frame. They believe that the Nuclear Installations Inspectorate is beyond politics – its evidence would be truly compelling. This logic separates government (the NII's paymaster) and industry, which the unemployed conflate, and suggests the public interest can, without conflict, be built into institutional procedures. The unemployed give no evidence of sharing that belief.

In commenting on programmes' formal devices these groups notice the same things but evaluate them differently. Thus the unemployed seem to approve of overtly persuasive devices in *Uncertain Legacy* whilst the Rotarians object to being 'dragged through the nose' (sic) by it. *Energy – the nuclear option* attracts similar criticism from both groups whilst the (generally) hostile reaction to *From Our Own Correspondent's* 'playacting' by the Rotarians is not shared by the unemployed group:

(Unemployed)

It was a representation of a normal human being not someone who sits in an office all day waffling a load of facts ... You had somebody who didn't know what was going on ... I think it was the fact that they suddenly brought home that this could actually happen.

In summary: the dominant frame for the Rotarians is the evidential, for the unemployed, the political. The Rotarian's evidential discourse brings in their professional knowledge. The unemployed group politicizes in conflating government and industry as an unequivocally pro-nuclear interested party, as against the Rotarians' trust in the disinterestedness of certain institutions. Political differences at the level of 'pro' and 'anti' nuclear power map on to the groups negative/positive evaluations of persuasive devices in the programmes. The Rotarians privilege rationality over affect to a much greater extent than the unemployed, whilst 'environmental' framing is minimal for both groups.

3. Heysham workers and Friends of the Earth

Both these groups adopt a civic frame in order to identify the 'bias' of each programme. However, the idea that programmes should be balanced gives the Heysham workers hardly any critical purchase on *From Our Own Correspondent* beyond the registering of its extremeness: even an anti- nuclear viewer would find it, in their view, 'over the top'. Where the other two programmes are concerned, although both are 'biased' (in opposite directions) the bias critique is pursued more energetically in relation to *Uncertain Legacy*. Furthermore, those aspects of *Energy – The Nuclear Option* that were read as biased by all other groups (notably the Walden-Marshall interview) were not so read by this group. In this respect, Friends of the Earth are more even-handed. Although they are on the anti-nuclear side of the debate, they show concern for fair treatment of the opponents' case in *Uncertain Legacy* and *From Our Own Correspondent*, as well as for the pro- nuclear position in *Energy – The Nuclear Option*. Part of the motivation for this may be a desire to see the argument conducted so as to convince people less persuaded than themselves of the undesirability of nuclear power.

Evidential concerns are, for both groups, strongly articulated with these civic ones. So, Friends of the Earth are anxious about weaknesses of evidence and argument in *Uncertain Legacy*, and the Heysham group challenge particular perceived messages too. Yet the latter are often not notably more confident in counter-knowledge than other groups when challenging at the propositional level:

(Heysham group)

> *I would have thought that if there was an actual link they should be surveying the actual people that work in the industry, because surely we must be getting a fractionally higher dose than the people are outside.*

Both personally-framed and environmentally-framed responses occur more directly in Friends of the Earth's account than they do in that of the Heysham group. Personal reactions of pleasure/displeasure in all groups are generally constructed, through group talk, into more impersonal critical positions. One Friends of the Earth member however, often adopts what we have called a personal framing by making intuitively-felt reaction the basis of her critical position. This does not happen in the Heysham group.

The environmentalism which we have noted as a part of Friends of the Earth's discourse is not their major line of engagement with the programme. But it is important in suggesting how they conceive of the nuclear issue politically – on a global as well as a national scale. By contrast, the Heysham workers follow the programmes in adopting a primarily national perspective.

It is only *From Our Own Correspondent* which provokes this group into adopting a directly political frame, in terms which register politicization as illegitimate partisanship:

(Heysham group)

It's highly political isn't it? It's really just a political group, rather than the general public, is that sort of thing.

There are some noteworthy differences between the two groups in their reactions to the formal properties of these programmes. The use of *Weekend World* as a model, and the contrived character of the Walden-Marshall 'interview' in *Energy – The Nuclear Option* escapes the critical attention of the Heysham group. For Friends of the Earth, these devices are found particularly problematic. The former group reads *From Our Own Correspondent* as scaremongering. Its 'What if ...' scenario barely saves the storyline from being condemned as falsehood. One speaker is amused as well as angered, recognising the intended effects of certain images. For Friends of the Earth, any success the programme may have in provoking anxiety is to be approved: anxiety about nuclear power's potential effects is an appropriate point of entry to the issues involved.

In summary – for both groups, a civic frame predominates, articulated with an evidential frame. There is more variation of framing amongst Friends of the Earth, who occasionally introduce a personal and/or environmental perspective. The civic-evidential articulation in both cases connects with a tendency not to see themselves as the intended viewers. The Heysham group objects when programmes give the intended viewer a misleading idea of what 'insiders' like themselves believe to be the case. Friends of the Earth want the intended viewer to hear arguments which are robust against cross-questioning. The groups' strongly divergent reactions to the programmes at the formal level are perhaps the most interesting differentiating feature of their accounts.

Convergence

1. In the case of *Uncertain Legacy*, the major point of convergence across the groups concerns the tension within it as between, on the one hand, its relatively restrained explicit discourse and, on the other, a subtext of threat. The former emphasises uncertainty and inconclusiveness – played off the industry's claims of near-absolute certainty – rather than proven risk. The latter works by encour-

aging inferences of danger, particularly through the use of visual images. All groups react, in one way or other, to this dynamic.

One response, seen in the account of the Heysham group, is to privilege threat as the primary meaning. This group is in no doubt that the programme offers a conclusive anti-nuclear message, by mischievous exaggeration, manipulation and exclusion of evidence. Readings which follow the grain of the programme's 'you can't prove anything but consider these coincidences' line of reasoning can result in inferences such as the Labour group's 'it seems to be more than a coincidence' which take that line one stage beyond the point where the programme itself (explicitly) stops. In one anti-nuclear group, Friends of the Earth, there is an apparent reluctance to make this move, and a concomitant regret that the programme does not more conclusively show that the risks are real.

Even pro-nuclear groups like the Conservatives admit difficulty in resisting the conclusions towards which the programme points whilst leaving the viewer to draw them. What the Conservatives are able to do is to challenge aspects of the programme's rhetoric, particularly its visual rhetoric, as illegitimate reinforcements of anti-nuclear conclusions. We have quoted above their comment on the use of Hiroshima film footage.

Such observations regarding the 'subtextual' level feature not only in the responses of pro-nuclear groups like the Heysham workers and the Conservatives, but come also from more equivocal groups like the medical students, and from groups with anti-nuclear sympathies. The unemployed group's favourable assessment of the visual effectiveness of the Trawsfynnedd Lake sequence in *Uncertain Legacy* is an instance of this here. That they notice the treatment and have an interpretation of the intention behind it, is what they share with many of our groups. Approval of that intention is, unsurprisingly, restricted to groups which share the programme's critical view of the industry.

2. There was a clear convergence of agreement across all the groups about the unsatisfactoriness of *Energy – The Nuclear Option*. This was more suprising in groups like that from the Conservative Party, where predisposition towards the pro-nuclear case might have been expected to lead to a supportive reading. In fact, the only group to produce a consensus approval of this programme were themselves employees of the nuclear industry – the Heysham Power Station workers. Drawing on the material cited and discussed above, we can identify three principal reasons for the widespread failure of this programme:

(a) A rejection of the programme's *promotional* design, especially insofar as this imitates aspects of non-promotional television. Brian Walden, the presenter, is often the focus of questions about the programme's integrity as it attempts to connect with the discourses both of journalism and public relations.

(b)   A sense that important omissions (the problem of waste) and insufficient attention to alternative energy sources give the programme's case for nuclear energy insecure foundations. This connects with 1. above insofar as Walden was often seen as being over-assertive in his presentation ('telling not showing'). Clearly, many groups had an anxiety about safety levels which, far from being eased by this firm approach, was actually worsened. We have noted a number of times the phenomenon of the 'boomerang' effect, whereby a textual focus on safety actually led, via interpretative inversion, to increased viewer worries about risk.

(c) A negative assessment of Lord Marshall as the head of the nuclear, industry. This was based on a number of factors, including ideas about his non-scientific status and about his possible 'foreignness' (his unusual accent suggests this to some viewers) but there was a general interpretation of his contributions (both to this programme and to the other in which he appears) as under-argued and, indeed, 'flippant'. What was presumably intended as a projection of informal frankness clearly failed with most of the respondents we spoke to. In *Uncertain Legacy*, it was the exchange with the interviewer about his likely response to a waste dump being sited in his garden that attracted the most criticism. In *Energy – The Nuclear Option* it was perhaps his vivid (but rhetorically imprudent) description of the effects of the Chernobyl explosion, in the context of a denial that power stations were 'like bombs'.

The degree of rejection of this programme suprised us and it is difficult to assess how far it is primarily a matter of a suspect form being used (an imitation of 'impartial inquiry', involving performances assessed as poor) or how far the especially deep concerns of our viewers about nuclear safety would have made it difficult for *any* commitedly pro-nuclear programme to win approval. The more recent tack taken in nuclear industry promotion, towards highlighting the major environmental risks produced by fossil fuel use, may have provided a significant new factor in the 'public meaning' of nuclear energy which we were unable to monitor.

3. In reacting to *From Our Own Correspondent* our respondent groups converge in their admissions of interpretative difficulty. On the one hand, these are retrospective descriptions of 'on-line' interpretative trouble. That is to say, in talking to the researchers after the programme has finished the impression is given that the programme's puzzles of comprehension were resolved very shortly after these puzzles arose. There are no 'loose ends' in this type of accounting:

(Unemployed group)

> *It confused me as well ... at the beginning with Chernobyl and this Russian presenter. And I suddenly heard 'Hartlepool' and I thought 'hang on, that's not in Russia', you know, that confused me for a couple of seconds.*

On the other hand there are statements which refer to interpretative problems that the respondent has not resolved by the end of the programme, like whether all of the programme or only some of it is 'play-acting' (Rotary group) and the status of the final on-screen text (Individual respondent A, quoted in the section on other groups). Given the complexity of the programme's communicative design, it is perhaps not surprising that some of its moves are experienced as problems. We have described how the programme deliberately 'false-foots' its viewers by allowing them to entertain the belief that it is an authentic Chernobyl report, before revealing its actual status as a fictional Hartlepool one. The Chernobyl interpretation is retrospectively constructed as a *mistaken* one, and some respondents seem almost to believe themselves guilty of a misreading, even though they have simply fallen in line with the guiding intentions of the programme. It is worth drawing attention, by contrast, to what we would see as actual 'misreadings' – for example, when the speaker in the unemployed group observes that the programme's point would have been more effectively made by using people from Chernobyl.

It is interesting, too, to note those cases in which groups who themselves understand the fictionality of the scenario, speculate that other viewers may not – that there are no intra-textual clues, or not enough, to make its status obvious to all. The suggestion is that the programme-makers hope its viewers will take fiction for fact. There is a hint of this in the Heysham group but it comes through most clearly in the Conservative group:

(Conservative group)

> *A lot of it was fiction and unfortunately I believe that there are some people who would see that film and would really and truly believe that it had happened. I would be far more interested to know the organisation behind it and the use to which it is being put.*

Although our Phase Two study of *Heart of the Matter* was only conducted with three groups of viewers, it is clear that it was generally interpreted as suggesting a Sellafield radiation-leukaemia link, despite its drawing on explanations which problematized or even rejected this. Our own analysis suggested that it was, in basic structure, a two-level programme. At one level, it focussed on a particular instance of illness and the legal battle which was beginning around it. At another level, it engaged more broadly with questions of risk probability in the nuclear industry. But the sheer power of the depiction it offered of one family's tragedy, backed up the programme's own 'dark' framing of the industry (see our discussion in Chapter 3) tended to crystallise meanings at the lower level for our respondents, leaving the wider reach of speculation relatively unassimilated.

Indeed, there were indications that (not for the first time in our study) respondents were confused by the complexities and counter-hypotheses of expert testimony, preferring to stick with the causal claim which underlay the legal action, the main narrative dynamic of the programme. Once more, an official representative of the nuclear industry was seen to deliver an inadequate account – in this case, the adversarial edge on the questions asked by Joan Bakewell and the subsequent dimension of conflict introduced into the interview with the BNFL spokesman may have reinforced such an assessment. It is interesting that few of our respondents thought the legal case stood much chance in court. This was not by any means a reflection of their judgment on its rightness but the product of a cynicism about the relative power of a major industry against a single individual. Some of our student respondents politicized this view. Another factor at work here, though, was a difficulty with the idea of 'probability', despite the extent to which the latter part of programme opens out around alternative, plausible but conflicting ideas of cause. Only 'proof' will secure a legal victory, it is thought by most of our respondents, and the controversiality of the issue is projected by the programme with sufficient strength to ensure that most viewers do not think this will easily be forthcoming. (As we noted in Chapter 1, this programme takes its primary material from precisely that area which has seen the most important development in the 'risk' debate since we conducted our research – the statistical findings of Professor Martin Gardner concerning the incidence of leukaemia among the families of Sellafield workers.)

Dynamics of interpretation and response

It should be apparent that in the foregoing accounts of our respondent groups we are offering analytic interpretations of the talk produced during group discussions. More is involved than simply reporting what was said in the course of each session. We have tried to quote from the sessions as fully as possible, but the reason for this is not to provide abbreviated transcripts. Rather the quotations, and the comments which surround them, are intended to exemplify the analytic approach we have taken.

We have made an effort to cover the following points in the case of the nine groups covered in detail. Firstly, we have tried to characterise the interpretative positions of the group as a whole. Secondly, we have singled out for special comment any individual speakers whose responses differ significantly from those of the rest of the group. Thirdly, we have attended to the ways in which readings are collectively produced, involving the negotiation of meanings amongst group members; consequently, and fourthly, we have attended to the dimension of *time* in these group accounts. Initial reactions are in all cases developed and modified as the event progresses and, in Phase One, as each new programme introduces new comparative possibilities.

We have thus sought in our methods to avoid potential mistakes in interpretation of the data. We have been cautious about taking the remarks of a single respondent to stand for the group as a whole and only done so when other evidence supported that judgment. We have recognised the potential for a 'consensus effect' whereby individuals are drawn into a group consensus for reasons to do with group dynamics, so that aspects of their responses which do not 'fit' the consensus are marginalized by the ongoing talk. And we have not taken early comments as the definitive final word on a programme.

Some exemplification of these four points is in order. The first two are best taken together. The nine groups which we have considered separately were chosen for this treatment out of the full range of sixteen precisely because they were the ones which seemed to us to be most characterisable in group terms, notwithstanding divergences within them which we have, of course, addressed as we perceived them. Such features as the Labour group's distrust of official pronouncements, the Rotarian's desire for scientifically authoritative information, and the unemployed group's foregrounding of a political framework of interpretation, were strongly endorsed within the respective groups. However, to take an example of divergence, it was notable in the Heysham group that one speaker in particular was more nervous about the question of risk than the others. It was also apparent that another of the speakers in that group wanted to talk more about visual and affective meaning, such as the intended effects of the Trawsfynnedd Lake sequence in *Uncertain Legacy*, than the others did. The result was that although he got to make his points, and to receive assent for them in the talk, they were not picked up for amplification by others; nor did anyone else offer spontaneous observations of a similar kind.

The collective, negotiated production of meaning in groups is nicely illustrated by the unemployed group where, as we have described, the interpretative positions adopted by speakers C and B in response to *Uncertain Legacy* are initially negative and positive respectively, with C's criticisms, mounted from within a civic perspective, concerned with its lack of impartiality. In reacting to B's more favourable assessment, whilst hanging on to his own initial perception of bias, C later came to the conclusion that the programme should have been more explicit about its basic anti-nuclear stance. A comparable case occurs within the Labour group where one speaker's more equivocal position on the nuclear issue itself correlated with a more critical reading of *Uncertain Legacy* and a less critical one of *Energy – The Nuclear Option* than the other group members. Negotiating this divergence often contributed substantially to the group's sense of direction.

Apart from these opportunities for amplification and negotiation, the major effect of the time dimension upon the results of the study is that respondents had three programmes screened in a given sequence. One consequence of this was a tendency to perceive the first two programmes as equivalents: the second is said by the Conservative group to be as biased in favour of the industry as the first was against it. Alternatively, either programme can be used as a framework and the other one read within the terms of that framework, so that *Energy – The Nuclear Option* can be read as 'leaving out' certain important things, because those were the things *Uncertain Legacy* had included (the waste issue, for example). This logic works the other way too. For the unemployed group, the screening of the second programme provokes the comment that the argument about the future necessity of nuclear power was omitted from *Uncertain Legacy*. Some groups are themselves sensitive to the comparison-effect upon their evaluations and reflexively draw attention to this.

The hardest thing to monitor in analysing this data is the *situational* consensus-effect. There is no way of knowing what any individual would have said in the context of a one-to-one discussion with a researcher, or in a group with a different orientation. In practice, we assumed that this effect would be most likely to come into play around the margins of debate, and that speakers would be unlikely to *abandon* their principal responses for the sake of consensus. Occasionally, we noticed traces of doubt too weak to take the form of explicit resistance to consensus. For instance, in the Rotary group a speaker with some professional loyalty to the nuclear industry goes along with the group critique of *Energy – The Nuclear Option's* communicative design, whilst showing a desire to protect aspects of that programme's substance from attack.

Conclusion

In this final section of our account we want to summarise the main points which have emerged from our inquiries. Given the range of issues upon which we have offered analysis and commentary, the points should not be seen as the 'findings' to which the preceding chapters stand as 'evidence' (each chapter argues its own local conclusions) but rather as an attempt at bringing out concisely the more significant features of our work.

If we start by considering what the implications of our case-study might be at the level of the general (and increasingly international) debate about television and public culture, then connection and development is strongest at four points of the inquiry.

First of all, the 'comparative textualization' aspect of our study has thrown into relief elements both of the rhetorical design and local usage of TV's *expositional* discourse. With the exception of studies of the news, this area of television has been relatively neglected in the research literature despite its centrality to the medium's public information role.

By taking a topic which has both scientific and general political aspects, our study illustrates some of the difficulties, of visualization and of appropriate speech, which characterize television's expositional narratives in the search for combinations of clarity, fairness and good 'viewability'. Some options and problems for more partisan formats are also identified. In the context of increased media attention to health and environment issues ranging from global warming to methods of food production – attention in which 'story-values', quite apart from individual disposition, tend to place TV journalists in implicit opposition to government and industry – this kind of investigation deserves to be developed.

Our study has also connected with 'influence' arguments, particularly insofar as we have registered the extent to which television images can exert a 'positioning' power upon viewer imagination and understanding of a kind which may prove more resistant to counter-interpretation than the devices of commentary, interview and voice-over. Viewers more readily naturalize images as unmediated since, unless they presume a general *intentionality* behind the overall pattern of visual depiction, they are not generally provoked to reflect on, and deconstruct, specific representations. We comment further on the 'influence' agenda below.

Whereas 'influence' suggests a top-down process, our study (in line with much recent audience research) has also emphasized the active and differentiated processes of interpretation. Here, the disposition of viewing groups towards the televised accounts, varied as it is (among other things, by group affiliation) shows a considerable degree of fairness-seeking and the exercising of 'civic' consciousness. This offers some check to those theoretical positions still making heavy use of theories of selective perception in which viewers are supposed systematically to disattend to that which does not coincide with their favoured viewpoints.

These factors – of expositional form, mode of address, visualization and viewer expectation – are combined, along with other elements, in what we might see as the Television and Citizenship issue. This is an issue running through much contemporary argument about television and is one likely to intensify as the long-running question about how market-based media systems can best enable democratic information-flow and debate is addressed anew in Europe. It is an issue in which the politically pessimistic implications of 'influence' theory connect up critically with some of the optimism and sense of potential deriving from recent 'active viewer' research, with both being put in the context not only of changing television forms but, often, of changing principles of political life. Our focus in this book is some way from that level of generality, but not so far as to prevent it from having a contribution to make.

We can now turn to some of the more specific points which have been documented and attributed significance by our research. It seemed best to consider first those points of rhetorical design and generic expectation holding some significance for a general understanding of 'public affairs' television, and then to move to points concerning nuclear energy and the particular mediations and interpretations which surround it. Such a separation of form from content exerts a distorting pressure both on the programmes and the responses to them, but the clarity thus obtained may justify this.

Our analysis characterised *Uncertain Legacy* and *Heart of the Matter* as *quests*, in which a strongly personalised journalistic 'mission for truth' is undertaken and in which the reporter's intervention into geographic, social and, as it were, argumentative space is often dramatized as ongoing action. This mode is a primary one within British public-service journalism and we identified some of its local devices for maintaining both thematic coherence and viewer 'watchability'. Perhaps the key point here concerns the specific forms of interplay between explicit (if also often ironic) verbal discourse and the richer, associative, sometimes directly symbolic, significations of the visualization. The articulations of an explicit even-handedness with an implicit critique which this permits seems to us to be caught by our research in a revealing and important way. We then analysed in detail the contrastive promotional tactics of *Energy – The Nuclear Option*, and developed an account of its imitative organisation (a 'pseudo-quest') and the discursive play-off between inquiry and persuasion which this entailed. The particular devices of ventroloquism and theatricality employed we find to be of considerable interest to an analysis of corporate audio-visual discourse and we believe that further useful work could be done in this general area as it continues to interconnect with the public forms of broadcast television.

From Our Own Correspondent raised general questions about the use, in public debate, of fully dramatised, imaginary formats to engage with more normatively documented accounts. Our conclusions here noted the problems of coherence and reality-status involved, particularly in using a mix of 'real' with 'imagined' information, and in emphasising emotional over propositional logics. Our formal analysis of all these issues of textualization relies extensively on the responses of the viewing groups as well as our own initial readings.

Responses, the major part of our study, are drawn together and made sense of in the last chapter, including a detailed patterning of programme-group convergences and variations, so further summarising here would risk unhelpful repetition. However, we would want to emphasise *the extensive presence in viewers' accounts of the 'civic' frame*, a frame which strenuously, and sometimes with great difficulty, seeks for overall 'fairness' above the weighted presentation of even a preferred viewpoint. Such a sought 'fairness' is massively problematized by its inter-articulation with ideas of balance and (more so) of truth, but it is the single most powerful regulator of interpretative assessments we found and it frequently provides the parameters within which a critical scrutiny of *forms* is carried out by the viewer. There may well be a strong topic-specific element at work here (i.e. you want fairness more when you're anxious and doubtful) but the scale and reach of such a civic consciousness is not the less interesting for this.

In our accounts of the programmes we noted how they variously engaged with and developed themes within the nuclear debate, accessing and framing both expert knowledge and experiential testimony to suit their distinctive rhetorical designs. The (un)decidability of contested points has a central place in the televisual textualization of the nuclear issue. This is represented both in epistemological and more political terms. Epistemologically, it is addressed as a question of 'proof' – for example, on leukaemia clusters. Politically, it is addressed as a conflict between interested parties – for example, on 'acceptable' risk levels.

The groups reacted to these indeterminacies in various ways, according to their own agendas of concern. The following points itemize what we would see as the most interesting features of the group accounts.

First of all, it was clear that respondents' own prior doubts and anxieties about the industry were widely shared – notably on waste disposal and leukaemia clusters – even by groups who might be expected to take a view more sympathetic to the industry. The programmes were playing into an interpretative context of deep uncertainty.

Secondly, we noted that uncertainty would often be *overlaid* by confidence, in either direction – the kind of confidence which is a matter of faith or hope, rather than specific factual knowledge. This led to patterns of critical attention to textual strategies as these were perceived against the background of the respondents' own preferred conclusions.

Thirdly, we noted that different groups attached differential value to the *affective* properties of televisual texts – potent visualizations, dramatic simulations, eloquent personal narratives. For some groups the nuclear issue positively requires such strategies, to win the viewers' involvement. Others argued the danger of allowing emotions, not reason, to decide the issue. Yet this striking *divergence* between the groups should not be allowed to obscure the more important *convergence* – the power of the affective dimension, even on groups who reject its legitimacy, comes through in many ways. This may be of considerable significance in the shaping of public opinion about the issue. This third point connects our study to 'influence and effects' questions. Work focussing directly on 'effects' has been widely criticised in recent years for too positivistic and functionalist a perspective, neglecting both the existence of intervening variables and the very nature of meaning-making. But there has been an opposite, and in our view equally unhelpful, tendency in cultural studies research over the last decade towards celebrating the 'plurality' of interpretation to such an extent as to push questions of 'influence' almost entirely off the agenda. Quite apart from the habitual tendency of this work to collapse questions of primary meaning into those of response,[19] it often entertains the idea of 'active viewers' crafting their significances from texts without any structured set of socio-cultural competences, options and limitations *bearing down* on what they do. We hope that our own work is not recruited to such a facile version of cultural 'liberation'. The 'influence' arguments continue, and though our findings suggest that, indeed, there is a good deal more at issue than many traditional approaches have assumed, they also suggest that taking the power of television seriously is as important as recognising the considerable extent to which it falls well short of being omnipotent.

In that that sense, we think that our research might further open up the research agenda to work which may, nevertheless, profitably differ from ours in scale, range of variables engaged with and relationships posed between formal and

---

19 *We have commented above upon the importance of this distinction. See the introduction to Chapter 4, 'The viewers'.*

substantive dimensions. A natural science model of cumulative knowledge developed via a research chain of 'carried-over' findings is an impossibility in the area of cultural analysis, but we think we have found out a number of important things about the TV process as well as about the public meanings of nuclear energy. Of course, it would be very satisfactory if, on reaching this stage, readers felt the same.

Selected Bibliography

We list below a few of the more important books and articles which relate to the inquiries in this book through either their substantive topics, their theoretical frameworks or their methods. We can identify four areas where further bibliographical information than is provided in the footnotes would be useful: Media, Public Opinion and Science; Nuclear Energy; Broadcast Current Affairs Programming and Audience Reception.

1. Media Public Opinion and Science

Baruch Fischoff, S. Lichenstein, P. Slovic, S. Derby and R. Keeney: *Acceptable Risk.* Cambridge, CUP 1981.

Anders Hansen and Olga Linne: Environmental issues and the mass media, in *Cuardernos de Communicacion* 96 pp 47-55, 1986.

Neil Ryder: *Science, Television and the Adolescent.* London, IBA 1982.

Roger Silverstone: *Framing Science: The Making of A BBC Documentary.* London, BFI 1984.

Lee Wilkins and Philip Patterson: Risk analysis and the Construction of News *Journal of Communication* v37 n3 pp 80-92 1987.

2. Nuclear Energy in Britain

James Cutler and Rob Edwards: *Britain's Nuclear Nightmare.* London, Sphere Books 1988.

Tony Hall: *Nuclear Politics: The History of Nuclear Power in Britain.* London, Penguin 1986.

Louis Mackay and Mark Thompson (eds): *Something In the Wind: Politics after Chernobyl.* London, Pluto Press 1988.

Walter C. Paterson: *Nuclear Power* (Second Edition). London, Penguin 1986.

3. Broadcast Current Affairs

Charlotte Brundson and David Morley: *Everyday Television:* Nationwide. London, BFI 1978.

John Corner (ed): *Documentary and the Mass Media*. London, Arnold 1986.

Richard Ericson, Patricia Baranek and Janet Chan: *Visualising Deviance: A Study of News Organisation*. Milton Keynes, OUP 1987.

Philip Schlesinger, Graham Murdock and Phillip Elliott: *Televising 'Terrorism': Political Violence in Popular Culture*. London, Comedia 1983.

4. Audience Reception

Peter Dahlgren: What's the Meaning of This? Viewers' Plural Sense-Making of TV News, *Media, Culture and Society* v10 n3 pp 285–301, 1988.

Birgitta Hoijer: Studying Viewers' Reception of Television Programmes: Theoretical and Methodological Considerations, *European Journal of Communication* v5 n1 pp 29-56, 1990.

Klaus Jensen: *Maing Sense of the News*. Aarhus, The University Press 1986.

Klaus Jensen and Karl Rosengran: Five Traditions in Search of the Audience, *European Journal of Commmunication* v5 n2-3 pp 207-238, 1990.

Justin Lewis: Decoding Television News, in Phillip Drummond and Richard Paterson (eds) *Television in Transition*. London, BFI 1983.

David Morley: *The* Nationwide *Audience: structure and decoding* London, BFI 1980.

Kim Schroder: Convergence of Antagonistic Traditions? The case of Audience Research, *European Journal of Communication* v2 n1 pp 7-31, 1987.

Ellen Seiter, Hans Borchers, Gabriele Kreutzner and Eve-Maria Warth (eds): *Remote Control: Television, audiences and cultural power*. London, Routledge 1989.

Other Titles Available from John Libbey

ACAMEDIA RESEARCH MONOGRAPHS

Satellite Television in Western Europe
Richard Collins
Hardback ISBN 0 86196 203 6

Beyond the Berne Convention
Vincent Porter
Hardback ISBN 0 86196 267 2

The Media Dilemma: Freedom and Choice or Concentrated Power?
Gareth Locksley
Hardback ISBN 0 86196 230 3

Nuclear Reactions: A Study in Public Issue Television
John Corner, Kay Richardson and Natalie Fenton
Hardback ISBN 0 86196 251 6

Transnationalization of Television in Europe
Preben Sepstrup
Hardback ISBN 0 86196 280 X

BBC ANNUAL REVIEWS

Annual Review of BBC Broadcasting Research: No. XV - 1989
Peter Menneer (ed)
Paperback ISBN 0 86196 209 5

Annual Review of BBC Broadcasting Research: No. XVI - 1990
Peter Menneer (ed)
Paperback ISBN 0 86196 265 6

BROADCASTING STANDARDS COUNCIL MONOGRAPHS

A Measure of Uncertainty: The Effects of the Mass Media
Guy Cumberbatch and Dennis Howitt
Foreword by Lord Rees-Mogg
Hardback ISBN 0 86196 231 1

Other Titles Available from John Libbey

IBA TELEVISION RESEARCH MONOGRAPHS

Teachers and Television
Josephine Langham
Hardback ISBN 0 86196 264 8

Godwatching: Viewers, Religion and Television
Michael Svennevig, Ian Haldane, Sharon Spiers and Barrie Gunter
Hardback ISBN 0 86196 198 6 Paperback ISBN 0 86196 199 4

Violence on Television: What the Viewers Think
Barrie Gunter and Mallory Wober
Hardback ISBN 0 86196 171 4 Paperback ISBN 0 86196 172 2

Home Video and the Changing Nature of Television Audience
Mark Levy and Barrie Gunter
Hardback ISBN 0 86196 175 7 Paperback ISBN 0 86196 188 9

Patterns of Teletext Use in the UK
Bradley S. Greenberg and Carolyn A. Lin
Hardback ISBN 0 86196 174 9 Paperback ISBN 0 86196 187 0

Attitudes to Broadcasting Over the Years
Barrie Gunter and Michael Svennevig
Hardback ISBN 0 86196 173 0 Paperback ISBN 0 86196 184 6

Television and Sex Role Stereotyping
Barrie Gunter
Hardback ISBN 0 86196 095 5 Paperback ISBN 0 86196 098 X

Television and the Fear of Crime
Barrie Gunter
Hardback ISBN 0 86196 118 8 Paperback ISBN 0 86196 119 6

Behind and in Front of the Screen - Television's Involvement with Family Life
Barrie Gunter and Michael Svennevig
Hardback ISBN 0 86196 123 4 Paperback ISBN 0 86196 124 2